Camper's Guide to
INDIANA & OHIO
Parks, Lakes, and Forests
Where to Go and How to Get There

Camper's Guide to™
INDIANA & OHIO
Parks, Lakes, and Forests
Where to Go and How to Get There

Mickey Little

Gulf Publishing Company

Copyright © 1993 by Gulf Publishing Company. All rights reserved. Printed in the United States of America (color pages printed in Hong Kong). This book, or parts thereof, may not be reproduced in any form without permission of the publisher.

Gulf Publishing Company
Book Division
P.O. Box 2608, Houston, Texas 77252-2608

10 9 8 7 6 5 4 3 2 1

This title and graphic design are a trademark of Gulf Publishing Company.

Library of Congress Cataloging-in-Publication Data

Little, Mildred J.
    Camper's guide to Indiana and Ohio parks, lakes, and forests: where to go and how to get there/Mickey Little.
        p.   cm.
    Includes index.
    ISBN 0-87201-223-9
    1. Camp sites, facilities, etc.—Indiana—Directories.
2. Camp sites, facilities, etc.—Ohio—Directories. 3.
Indiana—Guidebooks. 4. Ohio—Guidebooks. I. Title.
GV191.I6L58   1993
647.94772′09—dc20   92-31304
                                                            CIP

Also look for these popular *Camper's Guides* at your favorite book store or camping/backpacking supplier:

Camper's Guide to British Columbia, Volumes 1 and 2

Camper's Guide to California, Volumes 1 and 2

Camper's Guide to Colorado

Camper's Guide to Florida

Camper's Guide to Michigan

Camper's Guide to Minnesota

Camper's Guide to Outdoor Cooking

Camper's Guide to Texas, Third Edition

Contents

Ohio

Region 1, 75

Region 2, 125

Acknowledgments

I am indebted to and wish to thank the following agencies for information—in the form of maps, brochures, photographs, telephone conversations, and personal interviews—without which this book would not have been possible.

Buckeye Trail Association
Indiana Department of Commerce, Division of Tourism
Indiana Department of Natural Resources
    Division of Fish and Wildlife
    Division of Forestry
    Division of Outdoor Recreation
    Division of Public Information and Education
    Division of Reservoir Management
    Division of State Parks
Mistix Corporation
Muskingum Watershed Conservancy District
National Park Service, U.S. Department of the Interior
North Country National Scenic Trail
Ohio Department of Natural Resources
    Division of Forestry
    Division of Parks and Recreation
    Division of Watercraft
    Publications Center
Ohio Department of Development, Division of Travel and Tourism
U.S. Army Corps of Engineers: Huntington, Louisville & Pittsburgh Districts
Wayne-Hoosier National Forests & all Ranger Districts

Sailing is popular at "no wake" lakes.

While every effort has been made to ensure the accuracy of the information in this guide, neither I nor the publisher assume liability arising from the use of this material. Since park facilities and policies are subject to change, campers may want to verify the accuracy of important details before beginning a trip.

Mickey Little

Photo Credits: All photos are by the author unless credited otherwise.

Winter may be the best time to view the wildlife.

Introduction

Because Indiana and Ohio share many things in common, it seems quite appropriate for this *Camper's Guide* to include both states. They not only share a common border, but the Ohio River borders both states to the south, and the state of Michigan borders both states to the north. They each border one of the Great Lakes: Indiana has 45 miles of Lake Michigan shoreline while Ohio has 312 miles of Lake Erie shoreline. With four distinct seasons, the climate of both states is generally temperate, but marked somewhat by extremes and sudden temperature changes. The first inhabitants of this region were the prehistoric Mound Builders, followed by many Indian tribes.

Geographically, Indiana and Ohio are also very similar. Indiana ranks 38th in total area while Ohio ranks 35th. Indiana has an extreme length of 280 miles and an extreme breadth of 160 miles; Ohio has an extreme length of 230 miles and an extreme breadth of 210 miles. The lowest point in each state is the Ohio River; Indiana's lowest point is 320 feet and Ohio's lowest point is 433 feet. The highest point in Indiana is near Bethel (1,257 feet) and the highest point in Ohio is near Bellefontaine (1,549 feet).

Indiana has three distinct land regions: the heavily glaciated north, marked by moraines and numerous lakes, including Lake Michigan with its beaches and fragile sand dunes; the flat plain of the central region that slopes toward the southwest; and the southern region, characterized by hills, ridges, knolls, caves, sinkholes, and waterfalls. This southern region, the foothills of the Cumberland Mountains, has the most striking scenery in the state.

Four land regions make up the state of Ohio: the Appalachian Plateau makes up almost all of the eastern half; the fertile Till Plain constitutes the bulk of the western half; a 5-to-50-mile-wide strip of the Great Lakes Plain borders Lake Erie; and in the south, an extension of Kentucky's Bluegrass Region forms a small wedge between the plateau and the lowlands. Glaciers planed the state almost level, except in the southeast, where narrow, forested valleys, steep hills, caves, and other striking rock formations are found.

The diversity of the land makes Indiana and Ohio exciting for the native folks and out-of-state visitors. And, speaking of visitors, keep in mind that both states have numerous visitor centers to assist you in your travel plans. Indiana has 23 convention and visitors bureaus located throughout the state. Ohio has 19 travel information centers located off major routes throughout Ohio, with 14 of the centers open year-round. Contact the state's Division of Tourism for the locations of these bureaus/centers. If requested, Tourism will also send you the state map and other travel information. Addresses and phone numbers are located in the Appendix.

Breaking Indiana's "Time Barrier." Perhaps, Indiana's Division of Tourism will also send you some information that explains the differences in "time" in various counties in the state. Some "natives" still have problems, so it's easy to understand why out-of-state visitors are often confused.

STATE FACTS

	Indiana	**Ohio**
Capital:	Indianapolis	Columbus
Nickname:	Hoosier State	Buckeye State
Entered Union:	December 11, 1816 (19th)	March 1, 1803 (17th)
Area:	36,185 square miles; ranks 38th	41,330 square miles; ranks 35th
Population:	5,556,000; ranks 14th	10,855,000; ranks 7th
State Motto:	The Crossroads of America	With God All Things Are Possible
State Flower:	Peony	Scarlet Carnation
State Bird:	Cardinal	Cardinal
State Tree:	Tulip poplar	Buckeye
Time Zone:	Eastern Standard Time all year long for most of state	Eastern/Daylight Saving Time

Notice that the "State Facts" chart indicates that Eastern Standard Time is used all year long for *most* of the state. There are a few exceptions to this rule. Simply stated, remember: there are six counties in the northeast near Gary and five counties in the southwest around Evansville that observe Central Standard Time in winter and Central Daylight Time in summer; then, there are five counties along the Ohio River and the Ohio border in the southeast that observe Eastern Standard Time in the winter and Eastern Daylight Time in the summer. Now, all you have to do is interpret this in terms of what "time" is being observed by most of the counties in the state! Wow! Are you still with me?

Consider these facts: the state and federal agencies in Indiana and Ohio offer more than 23,000 individual campsites at developed campgrounds, and camping facilities are provided at 76 state parks, 9 state fish and wildlife areas, 21 lakes, 13 state forests, and 2 national forests. Think of the options that exist for outdoor recreation!

This *Camper's Guide* shows you where to go and how to get to the popular, well-known campgrounds as well as the lesser-used camping areas. The public campgrounds presented in this guide are provided and operated by state and federal agencies, and afford varied options for outdoor recreation: fishing, boating, canoeing, backpacking, swimming, sailing, picnicking, bicycling, horseback riding, water skiing, or walking along a nature trail. In season, you can also cross-country ski, snow shoe, ice skate, ice fish, or snowmobile. You can pursue your favorite hobby as a bird watcher, photographer, botanist, geologist, or naturalist. You may choose to rough it along a backpacking trail or enjoy all the comforts of home in a recreational vehicle. You can spend a day, a weekend, or an entire vacation doing what you like best, no matter how active, or inactive. Let's take a closer look at a few of the recreational opportunities available to the outdoor enthusiast in Indiana and Ohio.

Boating and Canoeing

Many dams and reservoirs have been built in Indiana and Ohio for flood control. Indiana's major lakes range in size from 741-acre Hardy Lake to 10,750-acre Monroe Lake. Boat ramps, marinas, day-use areas and campgrounds surround these lakes; they are water sports centers in every sense of the word. Ohio now has almost 81,000 acres of inland lakes; these provide unlimited recreational opportunities. The Division of Watercraft in the Ohio Department of Natural Resources distributes a very informative brochure called *Ohio Boating Areas*. The brochure, organized by counties,

lists all of the lakes 50 acres and larger, and in chart form presents the activities and facilities available at each lake.

Interest in canoeing has steadily increased during the past several years. The best information on canoeing in Indiana can be found in the 1987 revision of the *Indiana Canoeing Guide*, available for $4.00 from the Division of Outdoor Recreation in the Indiana Department of Natural Resources. The guide describes 26 canoeing trails on about 1,600 miles of rivers and contains maps, recommended access points, shuttle routes, and mileages for each trail. Information about canoeing techniques, trip planning, and proper river use is also included. A free brochure called *Indiana Canoeing*, is also available from the Division of Outdoor Recreation; it covers tips for safe canoeing, and names and addresses of canoeing organizations and canoe liveries. Canoeists should keep in mind that the banks of all rivers should be considered private property. Only a very small part of the river banks in Indiana are in public ownership.

Canoeing is also very popular in Ohio; the type of water recreation possible on Ohio's streams and

"For everything there is a season" . . .
. . . *a time for boating* . . .

rivers is quite diverse. Boaters can travel to any part of the state and find rapid and wild water as well as calm and scenic water. Many of these rivers have been preserved through the state's scenic rivers program. Scenic rivers are designated and classified according to the outstanding qualities a stream may possess. The Scenic Rivers Act provides three categories for classification of a river: wild, scenic, or recreational. Two of Ohio's rivers, the Little Miami and Little Beaver Creek, have also been designated to the National Scenic River program. The Scenic Rivers Program is administered by the Division of Natural Areas and Preserves of the Ohio DNR.

An excellent series of pamphlets has been developed by the Division of Watercraft in the Ohio DNR for boaters using small watercraft such as johnboats, canoes, kayaks, and rafts. Each of the seven brochures bears the title *Boating on Ohio's Streams,* but have different subtitles: *Laws and Safety, Northwest Section (#1), Southwest Section (#2), South Central Section (#3), Southeast Section (#4), Northeast Section (#5), and Ohio Boating Clubs and Liveries.*

These pamphlets should prove to be invaluable to anyone boating Ohio's streams. The *Laws and Safety* pamphlet provides an excellent overview: an Ohio map displays the five sections covered in the individual pamphlets; and a table lists 59 rivers/creeks and 13 forks/branches, and gives the length, water classification, and region for each of the waterways.

Biking, Hiking, Snowmobiling, and Horsing Around

Indiana. This state is serious about bicycling! Nearly 800 miles of roads through some of the state's most scenic areas have been surveyed and designated as the Hoosier Bikeway System. Eleven routes have been chosen to provide the best combination of riding surface, safety, services, and scenery for the bicyclist. Routes are marked by pavement markings, and trailhead signs have been installed at staging areas and at the end of each route. Guidebooks for each route provide detailed maps to aid in navigation as well as direction of travel at intersections, essential services along the way, and distances between landmarks. A free brochure entitled *Hoosier Bikeway System* displays the routes, lists names and addresses of bicycling organizations in the state, and includes an order form to obtain the guidebooks; the brochure is available from the Indiana DNR. The DNR's Streams and Trails Section in the Division of Out-

. . . and a time for snowmobiling.

door Recreation is charged with the responsibility of developing bicycle routes and other trails through its "Hoosier Trails" program.

Hiking enables one to enjoy trails of every description that wind through the scenic and diverse public lands of Indiana and Ohio. According to the *Indiana Recreation Guide* every state park, every state forest, and five of the lakes in Indiana have hiking trails. Hiking is also popular in the state fish and wildlife areas, but there are no marked trails. The Hoosier National Forest claims 24 miles of trails. Indiana also has designated backcountry areas and several long distance hiking trails. These are described in a brochure entitled *Indiana Hiking,* available free from the Indiana DNR. This brochure also gives tips for safe hiking, names and addresses of hiking organizations, and sources for trail maps.

Specifically, Indiana has three backcountry areas for primitive, backpack camping: Shades State Park, Patoka Lake, and Hoosier National Forest. The brochure recommends the following long distance trails as the ones in the best condition for the more adventurous who want an enjoyable, overnight trail experience. Some segments of these trails can also be conveniently used for day hikes.

▲ The Knobstone Trail is Indiana's longest footpath—a 58-mile trail following the Knobstone escarpment, the state's most prominent geologic feature, through Clark State Forest, Elk Creek Public Fishing Area, and Jackson-Washington State Forest. Two loop trails, one 6 miles and the other 8 miles, have been developed at the northern end of the Knobstone Trail. Primitive, backpack camping is permitted in the two backcountry areas the trail crosses, as well as along the rest of the trail within certain guidelines. A free Knobstone Trail map is available from the Indiana DNR; a detailed, water-resistant trail map sells for $1.00.

▲ The 35-mile Adventure Trail is a loop trail located in Harrison-Crawford State Forest and Wyandotte Woods State Recreation Area. Much of the trail follows the natural escarpments overlooking the Ohio and Blue Rivers and Indian Creek. Primitive, backpack camping is permitted in designated areas along the trail, and overnight shelters are also available. Contact the state forest or the recreation area for cost and availability of the detailed, water-resistant trail map.

▲ The Salamonie Trail is a 22-mile loop connecting the Lost Bridge West and East, and Mount Etna State Recreation Areas along the south side of Salamonie Reservoir. The trail is open for hiking April through November. Camping is available at campgrounds in the recreation area. Maps are available from the Division of Reservoir Management of the Indiana DNR.

▲ The Two Lakes Loop and Tipsaw Trails are located in Hoosier National Forest. A 13-mile trail connects and loops around Indian Lake and Lake Celina; a 7-mile trail loops around Tipsaw Lake. Primitive, backpack camping is permitted, and campgrounds are available. Trail maps are available from Hoosier National Forest.

▲ Approximately 75 miles of trails are available for hikers in the Charles C. Deam Wilderness in the Hoosier National Forest south of Lake Monroe. The trail is along oak-hickory ridges overlooking Monroe Reservoir and through beech-maple hollows. Primitive backpack camping is permitted. Information about the wilderness and a trail map is available from Hoosier National Forest.

▲ Two other trails, which can be completed in a day, are: the Ten O'Clock Line Trail connecting Brown County State Park and Yellowwood State Forest; and the Three Lakes Trail and Low Gap Trail that loop through the Morgan-Monroe State Forest and the Patoka Reservoir property's roadless area.

Indiana snowmobile trails are provided each year through the cooperation of local snowmobile clubs, the Indiana Snowmobile Association, and the Indiana DNR. Many of the trails are located on trail easements leased from private landowners. The trails are open in December, January, February, and March when snow conditions are adequate. There are trailheads at each trail for parking vehicles and trailers. Information about trail conditions is available after the first good snowfall from the Indiana Snowmobile Association at (219) 679-4006 (24 hours a day, updated as trail conditions change). Another number to call is the Department of Natural Resources at (317) 232-4002 (24 hours a day, updated at least twice a week for information about public snowmobile trails, ice fishing, cross-country skiing, and hunting information). Only registered snowmobiles may be used on the trails. Individual brochures on each of the snowmobile trails are available free from the Indiana DNR.

In Indiana, bridle trails are available in 8 state parks, 7 state forests, on the Hoosier National Forest, and at Salamonie Lake. Horsemen's camps are located at 5 state parks, 6 state forests, and at Salamonie Lake. The Hoosier National Forest has 4 horse camps and 106 miles of horse trails. Approximately 75 miles of trails are open to horseback riders in the Deam Wilderness on the Hoosier National Forest.

Ohio. The Buckeye State has its share of hiking and backpacking trails too! According to the handout from the Ohio DNR entitled *Ohio States Park Directory,* 61 of the 72 state parks have hiking trails totaling over 475 miles. In fact, 19 of the parks have more than 10 miles of trails. Burr Oak, Caesar Creek, and East Fork state parks have backpacking trails with backcountry camp sites; each park has a section of the Buckeye Trail. Although many of the trails in the state forests are designated as bridle trails, they provide the hiker with miles of walking pleasure. Fire lanes and unpaved roads, also may be enjoyed. Long-distance backpack trails have been developed at Shawnee and Zaleski state forests; Shawnee has a 60-mile backpack trail with walk-in camp areas, and Zaleski has a 23-mile trail with walk-in camp area.

The Wayne National Forest in Ohio has nearly 100 miles of hiking and backpacking trails. This mileage includes the 15-mile Wildcat Hollow Backpacking Trail, the 16-mile backpack trail at Lake Vesuvius Recreation Area, and portions of the North Country National Scenic Trail and the Buckeye Trail. Another long trail in Ohio is the Miami and Erie Trail; it is a 42-mile section of the Buckeye Trail that follows the tow-path of the old Miami and Erie Canal from Lake Loramie State Park north to Delphos. It is administered by the Division of Parks and Recreation; trail maps can be obtained from the Ohio DNR.

A variety of natural, scenic hiking trails are found within the 33,000-acre Cuyahoga Valley National Recreation Area, ranging from the half-mile loop trail at the Happy Days Visitor Center to the 13-mile Cuyahoga Trail maintained by the Boy Scouts of America. The best trail for backpacking in the recreation area is a section of the Buckeye Trail. However, at this time, there are no facilities within the park for overnight camping. Contact the recreation area for maps and information on the many trails administered by them; see the Appendix for their address.

At 1,200 miles long, the Buckeye Trail is not only the longest trail in Ohio, but it is also the longest continuous trail in any state. The trail is primarily a hiking trail; however, certain designated portions are open to other non-motorized uses. The trail is unique, among major trails. It completely encircles the state and follows a wide variety of terrain. The trail offers a wilderness experience in southeastern Ohio; in other areas, it follows abandoned railroad right-of-ways, old canal tow-paths, rivers, lake shores and flat farmland; it goes past or near many historic sites. It is often referred to as "The Walking History of Ohio." Camping is permitted only in designated areas. Waterproof, pocket-sized maps indicate the location of available campsites, on or near the trail, as well as approved sources of water. The trail passes through or near numerous state parks, state forests, lakes, and national forest lands. Public use of the trail is made possible through the cooperation of numerous agencies and the Buckeye Trail Association, Inc., a non-profit corporation made up entirely of dedicated volunteers. Membership dues and contributions are tax deductible. Contact them for information; refer to the Appendix for their address.

The 3,200-mile North Country National Scenic Trail begins in the Adirondack Mountains in New York and ends in the vast plains of North Dakota. It makes a U-shaped sweep through Ohio, and for much of its route, follows the Buckeye Trail. In March 1980, Congress passed the necessary legislation and created the North Country National Scenic Trail. The trail is a cooperative effort involving many agencies at all levels of government as well as private interests. At this time, nearly 1,000 miles of trail have been certified by the National Park Service. Certification indicates the segment is developed and managed in accordance with the National Trails System Act. Several major trail organizations assist the National Park Service and other public land managing agencies in developing,

protecting, and maintaining the North Country Trail. The North Country Trail Association was formed in 1981 to organize and coordinate the massive volunteer effort necessary for such an undertaking. This association works closely with the National Park Service in promoting development and use of the trail. Refer to the Appendix for their address. An informative and attractive color brochure on the North Country National Scenic Trail is available from the National Park Service in Madison, Wisconsin; see the Appendix for their address.

Ohio boasts bridle trails at 16 state parks totaling more than 340 miles; seven of these state parks have equestrian camps. There are also more than 100 miles of bridal trails located on state forests and wildlife land adjacent to other state parks. Wayne National Forest has one horse camp and 46 miles of horse trails.

Trails of every description wind through the scenic and diverse public lands of Indiana and Ohio.

How to Use this Camper's Guide

Each state is divided into two geographic regions, and the parks, lakes, and forests within each region are arranged alphabetically and are cross-referenced by name and city in the index. The first page of each region locates the park, lake, or forest on the map and gives the page number(s) where you can find more detailed information and maps of that specific area.

All the information in this *Camper's Guide* has been supplied by the respective operating agency, either through literature distributed by them, through verbal communication, or through secondary sources deemed reliable. The information presented is basic—it tells you how to get there, cites outstanding features of the area, and lists the facilities and the recreational activities available. Mailing addresses and telephone numbers are given in case you want additional information prior to your trip. For some parks, it may be a good idea to confirm weather and road conditions before heading out. Although most campgrounds are open year-round, keep in mind, that during the off-season, some camping areas may be closed or some facilities may be discontinued.

The maps showing the location of facilities within a park or campground should be of considerable help. These maps are usually available to you at the park headquarters, but they can also aid you in planning a trip to an unfamiliar park. Arriving at a park after dark can be tough if you don't know the layout of the campground. And, those of you who have attempted to meet up with friends at a predetermined spot at a large campground can read-

ily appreciate the value of having such a map prior to your arrival. Most parks are easily found with the help of a good road map, but vicinity maps have been included in some instances.

Because each ranger district within a national forest operates somewhat independently of the national forest as a whole, distributes its own materials, and in many ways has its own "personality" because of terrain, recreational opportunities, etc., information on each national forest is arranged by ranger districts. All national forest lands are available for primitive camping; those wishing to camp off-the-beaten path should consider purchasing the official national forest map, because even the best road map often does not show the many backroads in the forest.

The facilities at a campground are always changing, but a change in status usually means the addition of a service rather than a discontinuation. In other words, a camper often finds better and more facilities than those listed in the latest brochure. During the summer camping season, many parks offer interpretive programs, including nature walks, guided tours, and campfire talks, conducted by park personnel.

May this *Camper's Guide* serve you well in the years ahead, whether you are a beginner or a seasoned camper. Take time to camp, to fish, to hike, and backpack the trails, to become truly acquainted with nature . . . and with yourself, your family, and your friends! Don't put off until tomorrow what can be enjoyed today!

State Parks

The state parks in Indiana and Ohio are located in a variety of settings: on a river or inland lake, on the plains or the forested hills, or along the shoreline of one of the Great Lakes. Whatever the setting, those who enjoy camping should be delighted to know that more than 75 state parks allow camping and provide almost 14,000 individual campsites. In addition, many parks have cabin, lodge and inn accommodations, as well as group camps, equestrian camps, rally camps, and youth tent areas. These state parks provide the setting for a wide variety of recreational activities, but, needless to say, each park offers its own unique opportunities for fun and adventure.

This *Camper's Guide* contains detailed information on facilities and activities available at each state park. Each year various parks may upgrade and/or add facilities and services. To keep abreast of these changes, obtain the latest copy of the free park directory or recreational guide published by each state's Department of Natural Resources. You may also want to obtain the individual park brochure on any that you plan to visit; addresses and phone numbers are given. Only basic information about camping in the state parks in Indiana and Ohio is cited here.

Indiana

Indiana has 20 state "parks," ranging in size from 22-acre Bass Lake State Beach to 15,547-acre Brown County State Park. Eleven of these parks are located in Region 1 and nine are in Region 2. Nearly 4,700 individual campsites are available for family camping; three-fourths of the campsites are classified as "A" or modern sites with electrical outlets and modern comfort stations with showers and restrooms. Seven of these 20 parks have primitive sites available as well as modern sites; these primitive sites have pit toilets, and cost less than other sites.

Reservations may be made by mail or in person (phone reservations are not accepted) for all state parks, except Shades, Harmonie, Summit Lake, and Tippecanoe River, where all sites are on a first-come, first-served basis. The reservation period for most parks is from approximately the second weekend in May through Labor Day. Several parks extend this period into October and November. During the period when campsites are reservable, 50% of all campsites may be reserved for up to 14 days; others are available on a first-come, first-served basis. During the sum-

mer season, a minimum of Friday and Saturday nights is required for weekend reservations. For the three holiday weekends, Thursday night must also be included in the reservation. For details on reservations and fees of all types, request a copy of the latest *Indiana Recreation Guide* from the Division of State Parks in the Indiana Department of Natural Resources.

Several **permits** are available for those visiting the Department of Natural Resources properties. Instead of the daily admission fee of $2.00, an annual entrance permit is available for $18.00. This permit, good from January 1 to December 31, admits non-commercial vehicles, driver and passengers. For $5.00, Indiana residents 60 years old are eligible for the **Golden Hoosier Passport,** which admits them to all of the DNR properties that charge admission. A $12.00 annual boat launching permit, good for one calendar year, may

Most campgrounds can accommodate tents as well as trailers and RVs.

be purchased in lieu of paying the $2.50 daily launch fee. A $16.00 swimming permit is good for 20 admissions to any DNR pool instead of $1.00 daily pool admission fee.

Three **rent-a-tent sites** are located at Lincoln State park and 12 at Tippecanoe River State Park.

The rental fee includes a canvas tent mounted on a wood platform, camp stove, lantern, cooler, cots and foam pads, picnic table, and fire ring. **Canoe campgrounds** are available at Chain O'Lakes, Shades, and Tippecanoe River state parks; a **backpack campground** is available at Shades State Park. **Equestrian campgrounds** are found at five state parks: Brown County, Ouabache, Potato Creek, Tippecanoe River, and Whitewater Memorial. Tie-up for six horses is provided at each site.

Group camp facilities at six state parks offer accommodations for groups of 20 to 270 people. Basically, each facility offers sleeping quarters with cots, but no linens. Most have a kitchen and dining hall with utensils, dishes and restrooms/shower facilities. Churches, schools, scouts, and other groups use these camps because they are economical, versatile, and convenient. The state parks with group camps are: Lincoln, McCormick's Creek, Pokagon, Shakamak, Tippecanoe River, and Versailles. Wyandotte Woods State Recreation Area, located on the Harrison-Crawford State Forest, also has a group camp.

All but two of the state parks (Bass Lake and Summit Lake) have **youth tent areas** available for camping Monday through Friday. These areas are for groups with campers under 21 years old, plus adult leaders; groups include public groups, semi-public groups, and not-for-profit groups only. Camping is primitive: tent camping only, pit toilets, no showers, drinking water supply near the campground, fire ring and picnic tables. Reservations are required. Eight of the state parks have what is called **rally camping** for groups of five or more family camping units. Facilities are primitive and reservations are required; these areas are available Monday through Friday.

State park inns offer comfortable rooms, full service dining rooms, meeting and reception areas at six state parks: Abe Martin Lodge, at Brown County; Canyon Inn at McCormick's Creek; Clifty Inn at Clifty Falls; Potawatomi Inn, at Pokagon; Spring Mill Inn at Spring Mill; and Turkey Run Inn at Turkey Run. More than 500 guest rooms are available at these inns. Brown County, Pokagon, and Turkey Run state parks also have inn-operated cabins for rent. All inns take reservations two years in advance. To make a reservation call, write, or stop by the inn you wish to visit. A deposit equal to one night's rate plus tax must be received by the inn within 10 days after the reservation is made.

Family housekeeping cabins are available for rent at eight state parks, namely: Brown County, Chain O'Lakes, Harmonie, Lincoln, McCormick's Creek, Potato Creek, Shakamak, and Whitewater Memorial. The cabins offer privacy and comfort with bedrooms, living areas, kitchens, and modern bathroom facilities. The capacities of the cabins range from 4–8, depending on location. To make reservations for a cabin, it's best to call or visit the park; most parks accept reservations up to one year in advance. With the exception of Brown County, cabins must be reserved for either one or two weeks during the summer months and for a minimum of Friday and Saturday nights during spring and fall. Most cabins are open year-round, but several close in winter.

Many campgrounds are accessible to people who are physically challenged. If you desire such information, you may request a copy of *Access to Recreation—a Guide to Indiana State Parks and State Recreation Areas for the Handicapped Visitor,* by writing or calling the Division of Outdoor Recreation in the Indiana Department of Natural Resources.

Ohio

Ohio has 56 state parks that offer overnight facilities, ranging in size from 23-acre Lake White State Park to 17,229-acre Salt Fork State Park. Region 1 contains 29 of these parks and Region 2 contains 27. Over 9,000 individual campsites are available for family camping. Twenty seven parks have electrical outlets, 35 have showers and 27 have flush toilets. Five are located on Lake Erie: namely, East Harbor, Geneva, Kelleys Island, Maumee Bay and South Bass Island state parks. Five parks are located on a river: Beaver Creek, Independence Dam, John Bryan, Mohican, and Muskingum River. Great Seal is the only state park that does not have a measurable source of water, such as a lake or pond. There are 17 state parks located on lakes large enough to allow unlimited horsepower boating.

Campground **reservations** are *not* available in Ohio; all campgrounds are on a first-come, first-served basis except Mohican State Park, which uses a summer reservation system for the main campground. Preceding a holiday weekend, you may receive information on campground availability Wednesday through Friday from 8:30 a.m. to 5:00 p.m. by calling (614) 265-7000. For cabin and lodge reservations, call the park or lodge of your choice. For reservations during the summer, on holiday weekends, and peak fall color weeks, it is recommended that you call up to one year in advance. A deposit is required to hold your reservation.

Because **fees** are subject to change, campers and park visitors are encouraged to request the latest copy of the fee sheet, called *Overnight Facility Fees.* This sheet has current campground, lodge, and cabin rates. Special discounts on many facilities are available during the winter season. Throughout the year discounts are available to holders of the Golden Buckeye Card. Cardholders are given a 50% discount on camping rates Sunday through Thursday nights and a 10% discount on camping rates Friday and Saturday nights. Cardholders are also eligible for discounts on lodge and cabin fees. The Golden Buckeye Card is issued by the Ohio Department of Aging to Ohioans 60 years of age or older or Ohioans who are 18 years of age or older and certified totally and permanently disabled.

Rent-a-camp units are available at 13 state parks in Region 1 and 10 state parks in Region 2. Equipment includes an already set up 10-by-12 foot lodge-style tent with a dining canopy, two cots, sleeping pads, cooler, propane stove, and lantern, as well as a fire ring and picnic table. Electricity, showers, and flush toilets are available at many of the sites. For more information and an application, request the *Rent-A-Camp* brochure.

Equestrian campgrounds are available at 7 of the state parks; group sites are available at one park. The sites at East Fork have electric hook-ups, flush toilets and showers; the facilities at Beaver Creek, Caesar Creek, Deer Creek, Great Seal, Malabar, and Salt Fork are much more primitive.

Backcountry camping is available in four areas along the trail in East Fork State Park. Por-

Decisions, decisions . . . but at least the choices are visible.

tions of the Buckeye Trail and North Country National Scenic Trail pass through or near many of the state parks, thus giving access to the backcountry. In addition, four of the parks offer free of charge camping at designated primitive campgrounds. In some areas, water must be carried and many of the sites are referred to as "walk-in," located a short distance from the parking lot. The four parks with **primitive camps** are Blue Rock, Pymatuning, Scioto Trail, and Tar Hollow.

Group camps were created so that chartered organizations could participate in planned campouts. A small fee is charged. Reservations are necessary and can be made by phoning the park or camp office directly. Thirty two of the state parks have group camps; 16 are located in each region. Camps at 14 of the parks are for youth groups only, 8 are for tents only and the sites are walk-in at eight parks. Additional information is given in *A Guide to Ohio State Parks,* a publication of the Division of Parks and Recreation in the Ohio DNR.

Seven of Ohio's state parks have elegant **resort lodges.** From contemporary to Indian motif, each is unique, open year-round and a perfect retreat for the business group or entire family. Burr Oak, Deer Creek, Hueston Woods, Mohican, Punderson, Salt Fork, and Shawnee state parks offer a total of nearly 600 rooms, as well as dining, meeting, and recreation facilities. Each of the resort lodges has either an indoor or outdoor swimming pool; in fact, five of the lodges have both. Eighteen-hole golf courses are located at five of the resorts: Deer Creek, Hueston Woods, Punderson, Salt Fork and Shawnee. Reservations for each lodge, except Mohican, can be made by calling 1-800-282-7275. Mohican's reservations number is 1-800-472-6700. Meeting facilities reservations should be made by calling each lodge desk directly.

Several parks have unique **day-use facilities** that can accommodate your meeting or get-together. These range from rustic to more contemporary with a variety of arrangements and amenities. Some provide kitchen facilities or other features, and capacity varies from 30 to 150. Some are available all year, while others can be reserved on a seasonal basis. A nominal rental fee may be charged and will vary from site to site. Parks that offer day-use meeting facilities include: Hueston Woods, John Bryan, Rocky Fork, Quail Hollow, Caesar Creek, Lake Hope and Malabar Farm. Call the park office for more information and to reserve your meeting date.

Cabins in the Ohio state park system range from rustic to modern and offer many of the comforts of home. The locations of the 535 cabins are diverse with some hidden in deep woodlands and others with spectacular views of the large lakes. Cabin guests at parks with resort lodges have access to lodge facilities, except at Mohican, where the lodge and cabins are operated separately. There are several different types of cabins; most provide blankets, linens and towels. Modern cabins designed to sleep six, called **family housekeeping cabins,** are located at Buck Creek, Burr Oak, Cowan Lake, Deer Creek, Dillon, Hocking Hills, Hueston Woods, Lake Hope, Mohican, Pike Lake, Punderson, Pymatuning, Salt Fork, and Shawnee state parks. These cabins are available all year. **Standard cabins,** open seasonally from May 1 through September 30 or October 31, offer combination living and kitchen areas; they are located at Geneva, Hueston Woods, Lake Hope, Pike Lake, and Pymatuning state parks. Lake Hope has 23 rustic **sleeping cabins** with 1, 2, 3 and 4 bedrooms; they are available all year. The **Harding Cabin** at Deer Creek State Park, once a presidential retreat, sleeps seven and is heated and air-conditioned for year-round use. This cabin is rented through a lottery system.

South Bass Island State Park has four **cabents** for rent from Memorial Day weekend to October 1. Cabents (*cabin-tents*) are wooden structures with fabric roofs. Designed for a maximum occupancy of six people, they are compact, efficiency quarters consisting of one large room, a bathroom with shower, and a kitchen with stove, sink and a small refrigerator. Linens and cooking utensils are provided. Rental is on a weekly basis only and is done on a lottery drawing basis from the park's main office in Port Clinton.

Pet camping is permitted in designated areas in 40 state park campgrounds and in most equestrian camps. A fee of $1.00 per pet per night is charged in addition to the regular cost for camping. Pet camping areas are noted in this guide in the facilities list for each of the Ohio state parks.

The Division of Parks and Recreation is working toward modifying existing and planned facilities to make them more accessible to those who are physically challenged. For detailed information on accessible facilities, call the DNR at (614) 265-7000 or the park of your choice and request the *Special Places for All People* brochure.

State Forests

Although state forests may be used for a variety of recreational activities, that is not their main purpose. Their primary purpose is to produce timber, along with providing watershed protection, wildlife habitat, and forestry education. This multiple-use philosophy ensures that forest products will continue to be provided, as well as a place for people to get away from it all. Camping is permitted on state forest land only in areas provided and designated for such use. A fee is collected for camping at most state forest campgrounds, either at the entrance gate, at your camp site in the evening, or at a self-registration area.

In **Indiana,** the state forest lands that are available for recreational activities total almost 145,000 acres. Some 600 primitive campsites are available on 11 state forests. Primitive sites include a parking spur, picnic table, fire ring, pit toilet, and drinking water supply in the area. Three of the forests also have an area that is more developed for recreation along with a campground with modern conveniences. These areas are designated as state recreation areas, and include Deam Lake, Starve Hollow, and Wyandotte Woods. These three campgrounds have over 780 campsites with electrical

outlets as well as modern comfort stations with showers and restrooms. Reservations can be made at Deam Lake and Wyandotte Woods. Backcountry camping is available on four state forests: Clark, Harrison-Crawford, Jackson-Washington, and Morgan-Monroe.

State forests provide a place "to get away from it all"; in Indiana, some 600 primitive campsites are available in 11 state forests.

In **Ohio,** forests cover 26% of the land area and 65% of the forest area of the state is located in the southeast. The state forest lands that are available for recreational activities total over 173,000 acres. Although there are 19 state forests, only two of them provide family campgrounds. They are located on Fernwood State Forest and Harrison State Forest and offer a total of 48 campsites. The sites are primitive with vault toilets; drinking water is available. Harrison State Forest also has a primitive equestrian camping area with 25 sites.

Equestrian camping is also available at Maumee, Shawnee, Tar Hollow and Zaleski; Shawnee and Zaleski also have a walk-in camp along a backpack trail. The Buckeye Trail crosses five of the state forests: Hocking, Pike, Scioto Trail, Shawnee, and Tar Hollow. A portion of Shawnee State Forest is designated as a State Forest Wilderness Area. This *Camper's Guide* provides detailed information only on the two state forests with family campgrounds. For information on the other state forests, contact the Division of Forestry in the Ohio Department of Natural Resources.

State Fish and Wildlife Areas

Indiana has 41 fish and wildlife areas that are designed as multiple-use properties and offer a wide range of outdoor recreation activities. A variety of wildlife habitats (forests, grasslands, and wetlands) are also maintained on these areas that support both game and non-game wildlife. Although providing fishing and hunting opportunities is the primary purpose of these areas, other activities, such as wildlife viewing, picnicking, mushroom hunting, hiking, camping, and target practicing at a shooting range are found on many of the properties. Ice fishing is popular during the winter months.

Campgrounds are located in nine of the areas: five are located in Region 1 and four are in Region 2. Seven of the campgrounds provide primitive camping; these 236 campsites provide a parking spur, picnic table, fire ring, pit toilet, and drinking water. Almost 200 campsites are available at the modern campgrounds offered by Glendale and Willow Slough. Over half of the sites at Glendale have electrical outlets; all of the sites offer a modern comfort station with showers and restrooms. Willow Slough does not have electrical outlets, but it does offer a modern comfort station.

This *Camper's Guide* provides detailed information only on the nine properties that provide campgrounds. For information on the other fish and wildlife areas, contact the Division of Fish and Wildlife of the Indiana Department of Natural Resources.

U.S. Army Corps of Engineers' Lakes

The lakes and reservoirs in Indiana and Ohio were constructed primarily for flood control, but in addition to storing flood waters, these lakes provide a variety of outdoor activities associated with large bodies of water. These land and water areas are managed for multiple uses such as fishing, water-skiing, sailing, hunting, modern or primitive camping.

Indiana has eight lakes where the recreation facilities are maintained and operated by the Division of Reservoir Management in the Indiana Department of Natural Resources under a lease arrangement with the U.S. Army Corps of Engineers. The lakes are: Brookville, Cagles Mill, Cecil M. Harden, Huntington, Mississinewa, Monroe, Patoka, and Salamonie. At Hardy Lake, the smallest reservoir, the recreation facilities are owned and operated by the state; this lake was constructed by the Stucker Fork Conservancy District. Numerous boat ramps, marinas, day-use areas, etc. surround these 9 lakes; campgrounds are found at 15 of the state recreation areas. Nearly 3,500 individual campsites are available, with facilities ranging from luxury to primitive. Two of the recreation areas (Mounds at Brookville Lake and Miami at Mississinewa Lake) offer electrical outlets, sewage and water hook-ups.

Four of the recreation areas offer primitive sites only; these sites have pit toilets, but drinking water is available. Six other recreation areas have primitive sites available for those desiring them, but also have sites with modern comfort stations with showers and rest rooms. Nine of the 15 recreation areas have modern sites with electrical outlets; over 2,250 individual sites are available. Several campgrounds accept reservations at any time; others accept them for the three major holidays only. Huntington Lake is the only recreation area that is not on the reservation system. Refer to the facility list for each recreation area for information regarding specific facilities available. Addresses and phone numbers for the recreation areas are also provided, in case additional information is needed.

The fact that two of the lakes are known by different names often causes confusion. Lieber State Recreation Area is located on Cagles Mill Lake, which is also known as Cataract Lake. Raccoon State Recreation Area is located on Cecil M. Harden Lake and is known by both names. Also keep in mind that the water level in some reservoirs can change dramatically. This is especially true in the spring and early summer when there are heavy rains. High water can close down beaches, boat ramps, and some camping areas. If in doubt, be sure to call the property or DNR Public Information (317-232-4200) to check on conditions.

Ohio has numerous lakes constructed by the U.S. Army Corps of Engineers. Twenty-three of these lakes provide camping facilities as well as opportunities for other outdoor recreational activities associated with large bodies of water. Through a cooperative agreement, once a lake is completed, the recreational areas may be administered by other agencies. Such is the case with 11 of the lakes; they are now designated as state parks and are administered by the Division of Parks and Recreation in the Ohio Department of Natural Resources. The state parks at these lakes are: Alum Creek, Buck Creek, Burr Oak, Caesar Creek, Deer Creek, Delaware, Dillon, East Fork, Mosquito Lake, Paint Creek, and West Branch.

When visiting these lakes you will probably see the Corps office or visitor center, usually located near the dam.

An additional ten lakes are under the control of the Muskingum Watershed Conservancy District (MWCD). MWCD is responsible for all conservation and recreation throughout its 16,000 acres of water and 38,000 acres of land. Eight lakes have campgrounds: Atwood, Charles Mill, Clendening, Leesville, Piedmont, Pleasant Hill, Seneca and Tappan. All of the campgrounds at these lakes offer electrical hook-ups and all but two of them have flush toilets and hot showers; full hook-ups are available at several of them. The number of individual campsites available at these eight lakes totals nearly 3,000.

There are only four lakes where the recreational areas are operated by the Corps of Engineers: namely, Berlin Lake, Mohawk Lake, North Branch of Kokosing Lake, and the West Fork of Mill Creek Lake. There are over 500 individual campsites at these lakes; the combination of electrical hook-ups, flush toilets and showers are available only at Berlin Lake and West Fork of Mill Creek Lake. Golden Age and Golden Access Passports entitle the bearer to a reduction in federal user fees at Corps lakes.

Refer to the facility list for each lake for information regarding specific facilities available. In case additional information is needed, addresses and phone numbers are also provided. Remember that the water level in some reservoirs can change dramatically. High water can close down beaches, boat ramps, and some camping areas. If in doubt, be sure to call ahead before making the trip.

National Parks

The diversity of national parks is reflected in the variety of titles given to them. These include such designations as national park, national preserve, national monument, national memorial, national historic site, national seashore, and national battlefield park. Indiana has three such parks and Ohio has five. Although none offers camping facilities, you may want to consider including them in your travel plans. Each park has a museum or exhibit; with the exception of the International Peace Memorial at Put-In-Bay, each has a visitor center; several of them do require an entrance fee. However, keep in mind that the Golden Eagle Pass, the Golden Age Passport, and the Golden Access Passport allow free entry into the national parks.

Indiana Dunes National Lakeshore and Indiana Dunes State Park are adjacent to one another on Lake Michigan.

In **Indiana,** the Indiana Dunes National Lakeshore, near Porter, is in Region 1; George Rogers Clark National Historical Park at Vincennes, and Lincoln Boyhood National Mounument at Lincoln City are in Region 2. In **Ohio,** three parks are in Region 1: namely, Cuyahoga Valley National Recreation Area, that links the urban centers of Cleveland and Akron; James A. Garfield National Historic Site, near Mentor; and Perry's Victory and International Peace Memorial, at Put-In-Bay on Lake Erie. The two parks in Ohio in Region 2 are Mound City Group National Monument at Chillicothe, and William Howard Taft National Historic Site near Cincinnati. For brochures and other information on each of the parks, contact the National Park Service (see Appendix for address).

Federal Recreation Passport Program

Some federal parks, refuges, and facilities can be entered and used free of charge. Other areas and facilities require payment of entrance fees, user fees, special recreation permit fees, or some combination. A 1987 brochure by the U.S. Department of the Interior entitled *Federal Recreation Passport Program* explains the five programs. Briefly stated, they are as follows:

Golden Eagle Passport. An annual entrance pass to those national parks, monuments, historic sites, recreation areas, and national wildlife refuges that charge entrance fees. It admits the permit holder and accompanying persons in a private, noncommercial vehicle. For those not traveling by private car, it admits the permit holder and family group. Cost, $25; good for one calendar year (January 1 through December 31); permits unlimited entries to all federal entrance fee areas.

Golden Age Passport. A free lifetime entrance pass for citizens or permanent residents of the United States who are 62 years or older. Also provides 50% discount on federal use fees charged for facilities and services except those provided by private concessionaires. Must be obtained in person, with proof of age.

Golden Access Passport. A free lifetime entrance pass for citizens or permanent residents of the United States who have been medically determined to be blind or permanently disabled and, as a result, are eligible to receive benefits under federal law. Offers same benefits as Golden Age Passport. Must be obtained in person, with proof of eligibility.

Locations where these three passes are obtainable include all National Park System areas where entrance fees are charged, all U.S. Forest Service supervisor's offices, and most Forest Service ranger station offices.

Park Pass. An annual entrance permit to a specific park, monument, historic site, or recreation area in the National Park System that charges entrance fees. The park pass is valid for entrance fees only and does not cover use fees. Cost $10 or $15, depending upon the area; good for one calendar year (January 1 through December 31); permits unlimited entries only to the park unit where it is purchased.

Federal Duck Stamp. Officially known as the Migratory Bird Hunting and Conservation Stamp and still required of waterfowl hunters, the federal Duck Stamp now also serves as an annual entrance fee permit to national wildlife refuges that charge entrance fees. The Duck Stamp is valid for entrance fees only and does not cover use fees. Cost, $10; good from July 1 through June 30 of the following year; permits unlimited entries to all national wildlife refuges that charge entrance fees; can be purchased at most post offices.

National Forests

The 188,000-acre Hoosier National Forest is located in the rolling hills of southern **Indiana** while the 200,000-acre Wayne National Forest is located in the foothills of the Appalachian Mountains in southeastern **Ohio.** The Wayne National Forest is administratively linked with the Hoosier; the forest supervisor's office is located in Bedford, Indiana. Each national forest is divided into districts, with a district ranger responsible for multiple-use administration for the district. Hoosier National Forest is made up of two units and supervised by two ranger districts while the Wayne National Forest has three geographically separated units, but is supervised by two ranger districts.

Because each ranger district within a national forest distributes its own materials, and in many ways has its own "personality" because of terrain, recreational opportunities, etc., information on the two national forests in this *Camper's Guide* is

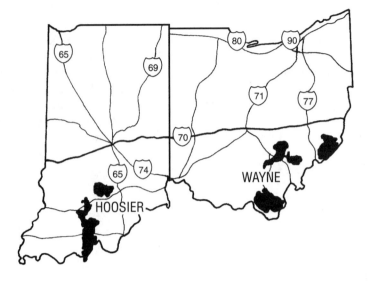

arranged by ranger districts. The best source for specific and local information is the district ranger's office administering the area. Visitors are encouraged to visit their office or contact them by phone or mail; for your convenience, addresses and phone numbers for these offices are included. They are able to supply you with brochures on the various recreational activities available, as well as give information on such items as campground accommodations during the off-season, whether reservations are available or required, road conditions, etc.

General information is given here. For specific information on campground locations and facilities, refer to the appropriate national forest ranger district.

▲ Ten campgrounds are operated and maintained by the four ranger districts, making available more than 450 individual campsites.
▲ Several of the more developed campgrounds offer electrical hookups, trailer parking, nearby piped water, and showers and flush toilets. Other campgrounds offer primitive campsites; these sites have a table, fire ring, tent pad, centralized water, and pit toilets.
▲ All national forest lands are available for primitive camping; those wishing to camp off-the-beaten path should consider purchasing the official national forest map, because even the best road map often does not show the many backroads in the forest.
▲ Backcountry rules are simple; pack out what you pack in, use campfires wisely, or better yet, use backpack stoves for fire safety. Water from springs, lakes, ponds, and streams should be treated. A recommended method of treatment is to boil clear water for five minutes.

▲ The Wayne-Hoosier National Forests offer more than 150 miles of horse trails and nearly 100 miles of hiking and backpacking trails. Other outdoor recreation that can be enjoyed on these lands includes fishing, hunting, boating, canoeing, cross-country skiing, snowmobiling, and viewing wildlife and wildflowers.
▲ Most campgrounds are open from spring to late fall, although services may be reduced in the off-season. Some are open yearlong (contact District Ranger for closures).
▲ The maximum limit of stay is usually 14 days. Camper user fees are collected at most campground entrances; some through a volunteer, self-registration system.

Recreational opportunities are unlimited on the Wayne-Hoosier National Forests; combined they encompass 388,000 acres.

▲ The majority of campsites are available on a first-come, first-served basis. A few forest campgrounds are on the reservation system with MISTIX; reservations are taken for a limited number of units at these campgrounds, so noted in this guide. A camp site can be reserved via check or credit card through MISTIX at 1-800-283-CAMP; an additional fee is charged for this service.

▲ Holders of the Golden Age or Golden Access Passport and their party are entitled to a 50% discount on fees charged for facilities and services at all national forest campgrounds nationwide, except those provided by private concessionaires.

▲ Three sites are available for group camping. Reservations are required and should be made with the respective ranger district. Four horse camps are available on the Hoosier National Forest.

▲ As a user of national forest lands, you have significant responsibility for your personal safety during any activity you might pursue. It is your responsibility to know the hazards involved in your activities and to use the proper safety procedures and equipment to minimize the inherent risks and hazards related to your activity.

The **Charles C. Deam Wilderness,** set aside by Congress in 1982, is 13,000 acres of national forest land southeast of Bloomington, Indiana. It is an uninhabited area of narrow ridges and steep slopes managed for primitive recreation and personal challenge. Mechanized vehicles are excluded. Approximately 75 miles of trails are available for hikers and are also open to horseback riders. Primitive, backpack camping is permitted. Visitors should be prepared to find their way unassisted. The wilderness is on the Brownstown District of the Hoosier National Forest; contact them for information.

Backcountry Ethics

Rules imposed by those who administer the various backcountry areas are actually common sense rules meant to control actions that may damage natural resources. Backcountry areas are visited for solitude and a "wilderness experience." Enjoying these areas also requires a commitment to preserve them. The U.S. Forest Service, National Park Service, and Bureau of Land Management have produced cooperatively a small booklet entitled *Leave "No Trace" Land Ethics.* They suggest guidelines for practicing no-trace ethics while traveling in the backcountry. These no-trace guidelines have been designed to better protect the land and lessen the sights and sounds of one's visit. Although these suggestions were written mainly for the hiker and backpacker, they are quite appropriate for anyone using the backcountry, whether traveling by foot, canoe, bicycle, or horse. Pick up a copy of this booklet from one of the agencies; only highlights are presented here.

General Information

▲ Bright colored clothing, packs and tents should be avoided. Consider choosing earth-tone colors to lessen the visual impact of your gear.

▲ Make an effort to stay on the trails; don't short-cut or cut across switchbacks. Trails are designed and maintained to prevent erosion.

▲ When traveling cross-country, spread out so that no new trails develop on their own. Avoid traveling through meadows and wet areas.

▲ Don't pick flowers, dig up plants, or cut branches from live trees. Leave them for others to see and enjoy.

Plan Your Trip

▲ Keep your party small.

▲ Take a gas stove to help conserve firewood.

▲ Bring sacks to carry out your trash.

▲ Take a light shovel or trowel to help with personal sanitation.

▲ Carry a light basin or collapsible bucket for washing.

▲ Check on weather conditions and water availability.

▲ Before your hike, study maps of the area, get permits if necessary, and learn the terrain.

Setting Up Camp

▲ Pick a camp site where you won't need to clear away vegetation or level a tent site.

▲ Use an existing campsite, if available. When campsites are designated, use them.

▲ Camp 200 feet or more from lakes, streams, meadows, and trails when you have a choice.

▲ Do not cut trees, limbs or brush to make camp improvements. Carry own tent poles.

Breaking Camp

▲ Before leaving camp, naturalize the area. Replace rocks and wood used; scatter needles, leaves, and twigs on the campsite.

▲ Scout the area to be sure you've left nothing behind. Everything you packed into your camp should be packed out. Try to make it appear as if no one had been there.

Campfires

▲ For a total no-trace campsite, you should cook on a stove and avoid building any fires.

▲ If fires are permitted and you need to build a fire, use an existing campfire site. Keep it small. Before you leave, make sure it is out.

▲ If you need to clear a new fire site, select a safe spot away from rock ledges that would be blackened by smoke; away from meadows where it would destroy grass and leave a scar; away from dense brush, trees, and duff, where it would be a fire hazard.

▲ Clear a circle of all burnable materials. Dig a shallow pit for the fire. Keep the sod intact.

▲ Use only fallen timber for firewood; small wood is best. Even standing dead trees are part of the beauty of wilderness, and are important to wildlife.

▲ Put your fire cold out before leaving, let the fire burn down to ashes, mix the ashes with dirt and water. Feel it with your hand. If it's cold out, carry the ashes several hundred feet from the campsite and scatter them. Replace the sod, and naturalize the disturbed area. If rocks were used, they should be scattered before leaving.

Pack It In—Pack It Out

▲ Bring trash bags to carry out all trash that cannot be completely burned.

▲ Aluminum foil and aluminum lined packages won't burn up in your fire. Compact it and put it in your trash bag.

▲ Cigarette butts, pull-tags, and gum wrappers are litter, too. They can spoil a campsite and trail.

▲ Don't bury trash! Animals dig it up.

▲ Try to pack out trash left by others. Your good example may catch on!

Keep The Water Supply Clean

▲ Wash yourself, your dishes, and your clothes in a container.

▲ Pour wash water on the ground away from streams and springs.

▲ Food scraps, tooth paste, even biodegradable soap will pollute streams and springs. Remember, it's your drinking water, too!

▲ Boil water or treat water before drinking it.

Disposing of Human Waste

▲ When nature calls, select a suitable spot at least 200 feet from open water, campsites, and trails. Dig a hole 6 to 8 inches deep. Try to keep the sod intact.

▲ Burn toilet paper when fire conditions permit.

▲ After use, fill in the hole completely burying waste. Then tramp in the sod.

Emergency Items

▲ According to conditions, carry extra warm clothing such as windbreaker, wool jacket, hat, and gloves. Keep extra high-energy foods like hard candies, chocolate, dried fruits, or liquids accessible. Don't overload yourself, but be prepared for emergencies.

▲ Travel with a first aid kit, map, compass, and whistle. Know how to use them.

▲ Always leave your trip plan with a member of your family or a close friend.

▲ Mishaps are rare, but they do happen. Should one occur, remain calm. In case of an accident, someone should stay with the injured person. Notify the nearest state, local, or federal law enforcement office for aid.

Practicing a no-trace ethic is very simple if you remember two things:

▲ Make it hard for others to see you.

▲ Leave no trace of your visit.

Several state parks in Indiana and Ohio have scenic waterfalls; this one is at McCormick's Creek State Park in Indiana.

Indiana
Region 1

INDIANA
REGION 1

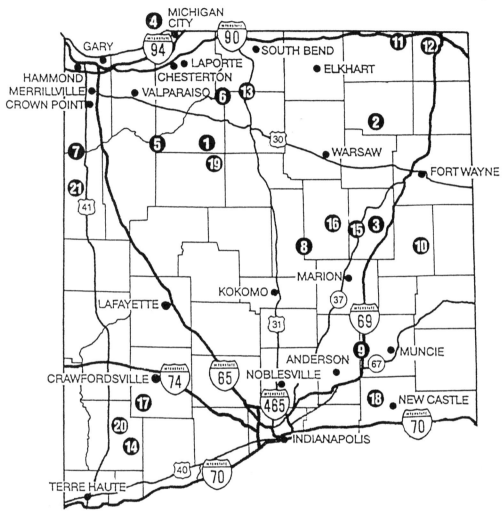

MICHIGAN
CITY

GARY

SOUTH BEND

HAMMOND
MERRILLVILLE
CROWN POINT

LAPORTE
CHESTERTON
VALPARAISO

ELKHART

WARSAW

FORT WAYNE

LAFAYETTE

MARION

KOKOMO

MUNCIE

ANDERSON
NOBLESVILLE

CRAWFORDSVILLE

NEW CASTLE

INDIANAPOLIS

TERRE HAUTE

Bass Lake State Beach

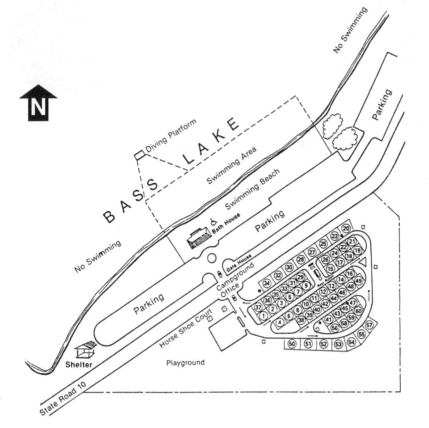

DS		Dumping Station
46		Electricity at Site
●		Water
▫		Garbage Receptical
♿		Usable by Handicapped

For Information

Bass Lake State Beach
Route 5
Knox, IN 46534
(219) 772-3382 (summer)

Location

Bass Lake State Beach is located south of Knox and east of U.S. 35 on S.R. 10. The 22-acre park, open from the Saturday before Memorial Day to Labor Day, is located on Indiana's fourth largest natural lake. Bass Lake contains 1,345 acres and 11 miles of shoreline; it is just under 3 miles long and is nearly a mile wide in a few places. Although the lake has a maximum depth of 30 feet, over half is shallower than 7 feet, and one-third is shallower than 5 feet.

Facilities & Activities

60 Class A campsites
   electrical outlets
   modern restrooms & showers
campground reservation system
dumping station
picnicking, 2 picnic shelters
playground equipment
swimming beach, bathhouse
fishing
motorboating, boat ramp (nearby)
designated boat-anchor area
waterskiing

Bass Lake State Beach does not have a boat launch facility, but one is located nearby.

Chain O'Lakes State Park

For Information

Chain O'Lakes State Park
2355 E. 75 South
Albion, IN 46701
(219) 636-2654

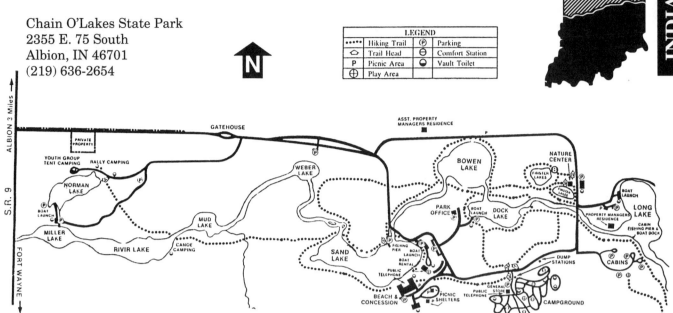

Location

Chain O'Lakes State Park is located northwest of Fort Wayne via U.S. 33 and S.R. 9, and southeast of Albion. Within its boundaries are 2,678 acres, including 212 surface acres of water and more than 7 miles of widely varying shoreline. The park, about a mile wide and 4 miles long, has 11 lakes that were formed by the last glaciers in this area approximately 10,000 years ago. Eight of the lakes are connected by channels.

Facilities & Activities

333 Class A campsites
   electrical outlet
   modern restrooms & showers
49 Class B campsites
   modern restrooms & showers
33 Class C campsites
   pit toilet
campground reservation system
dumping station
camp store
240-site youth tent area
60-site rally campground
canoe campground
18 family housekeeping cabins (each sleeps 6)
nature center, naturalist services

picnicking, 2 picnic shelters
playground equipment
swimming beach, bathhouse
beach refreshment stand
fishing, fishing piers, ice fishing
boating (electric motors only)
boat ramps
canoe/rowboat/paddleboat rental
7½ miles of hiking trails
cross-country skiing, ski rental
ice skating, sledding

Chain O'Lakes' swimming beach is located at Sand Lake, one of 11 lakes at the state park.

Huntington Lake

Kilsoquah State Recreation Area

Little Turtle State Recreation Area

For Information

Huntington Lake
517 North Warren Road
Huntington, IN 46750
(219) 468-2165

Faster! Faster!

Location

Huntington Lake is located on the Wabash River south of U.S. 224, west of I-69, and east of S.R. 5. Huntington Lake has 2 recreation areas: Kilsoquah and Little Turtle. Because Kilsoquah State Recreation Area and Kilsoquah Campground are adjacent to each other, the chart displays the combined facilities and activities. These 2 areas are off of U.S. 224—about 2 miles east of Huntington and 6 miles west of I-69 (exit 86). Little Turtle State Recreation Area is about ½ mile south of the Huntington Dam and to the left off S.R. 5; the state office is also on S.R. 5 on the left.

Huntington Reservoir operates primarily as a unit with Mississinewa and Salamonie Reservoirs to control flood waters along the Wabash River Basin. The lake and environs comprise 8,322 acres; at the summer pool level of 749-foot elevation, water forms a 900-acre lake with a pool length of 7 miles. The Huntington Reservoir property and surrounding area belonged to the Miami Indians when the white men first came to the area. Little Turtle, the greatest war chief of the Miami Indians, led much of the early resistance. Kilsoquah, Little Turtle's granddaughter, was born in 1810 about 5 miles downstream from the site of the Huntington dam. Referred to as the "Indiana Princess," she lived to be over 100 years old.

Facilities & Activities

	Kilsoquah SRA	Little Turtle SRA
Class C campsites pit toilets	100	30
youth tent area (100 sites)	X	
naturalist services	X	X
picnicking, picnic shelters	X	X
playground equipment	X	X
radio-controlled model airport		X
archery range		X
exercise trail/ball diamond	X	
swimming beach		X
bathhouse/concessions		X
hunting, fishing, ice fishing	X	X
boating/waterskiing	X	X
boat ramp	X	X
hiking trails	X	X

Indiana Dunes State Park

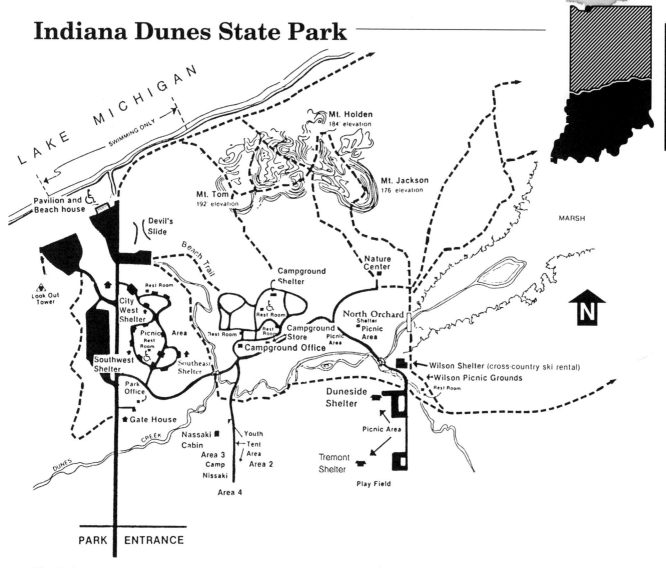

For Information

Indiana Dunes State Park
1600 N. 25 E.
Chesterton, IN 46304
(219) 926-1952 (park)
(219) 926-4520 (camp/ski)

Location

Indiana Dunes State Park is located midway between Gary and Michigan City, 2 miles north of I-94 on S.R. 49. The 2,182-acre park includes more than 3 miles of Lake Michigan's south shoreline. Eighteen hundred acres are wooded and contain the most diversified flora and fauna of the midwest; other areas are peculiar to the dunes region. The 9.2-mile Calumet Bike Trail borders the park, running along a utility corridor; it parallels U.S. 12 and connects the park to the Indiana Dunes National Lakeshore.

Facilities & Activities

121 Class A campsites
    electrical outlet
    modern restrooms & showers
187 Class B campsites
    modern restrooms & showers
campground reservation system
dumping station
camp store, snack bar pavilion
150-site youth tent area
nature center, naturalist services
picnicking, 6 picnic shelters
enclosed shelter (year-round rental)
playground equipment
swimming beach, bathhouse
access to 9.2-mile Calumet Bike Trail
10 hiking trails totaling 16½ miles
cross-country skiing, ski rental

Jasper-Pulaski State Fish & Wildlife Area

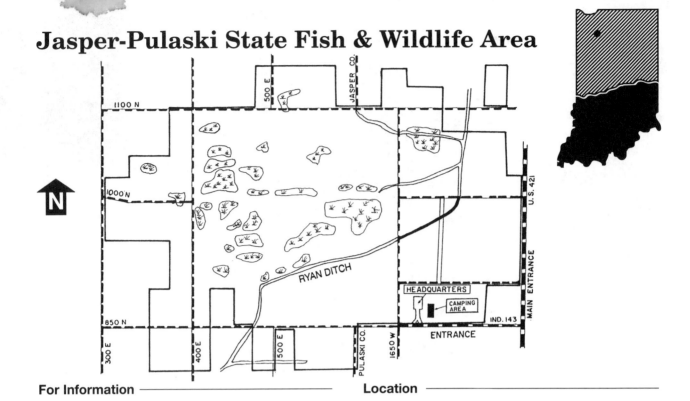

For Information

Jasper-Pulaski State Fish & Wildlife Area
R.R. #1, Box 166
Medaryville, IN 47957
(219) 843-4841

Location

Jasper-Pulaski State Fish & Wildlife Area is located west of U.S. 421; from the small town of Medaryville travel north for about 4 miles, then west on S.R. 143 for 1½ miles to the property headquarters. The camping area is adjacent to headquarters. Jasper-Pulaski features 8,022 acres of wetlands and upland game habitats. With 2,000 acres of wetlands, it is home to a large population of Canada geese. Because of suitable habitat, the property has become a major stopover point for migratory birds, including the sandhill crane. More than 10,000 cranes stop during the fall migration, and a large number also use the property during the spring. Jasper-Pulaski is a great area for viewing wildlife; observation towers are available.

Facilities & Activities

51 Class C campsites
   pit toilets
water, picnic tables & grills
picnicking
shoreline fishing, ice fishing
hunting
shooting, archery range
berry, mushroom, nut gathering
hiking trails

Opportunities for nature study are numerous at the fish and wildlife areas.

Kingsbury State Fish & Wildlife Area

For Information

Kingsbury State Fish & Wildlife Area
5344 South Hupp Rd.
LaPorte, IN 46350
(219) 393-3612

Location

Kingsbury State Fish & Wildlife Area is located 9 miles southeast of LaPorte. The area headquarters is accessible off S.R. 104 at Stillwell, or east of U.S. 35 (at the U.S. 6 intersection) on County Road 500S. Headquarters is on Hupp Road; the camping area is about 1 mile north on Stillwell Road. This 6,059-acre property is bordered by the Kankanee River on the southeast. The 15-acre Tamarack Lake is flooded seasonally into the 100-acre Tamarack Marsh. South of this, the Grande Marsh is flooded in the fall to about 300 acres. Tagged deer may be seen on the property and are part of a deer movement study being conducted at Kingsbury.

Opportunities to view wildlife are equally abundant.

Facilities & Activities

18 Class C campsites
  pit toilets
water, picnic tables & grills
picnicking
fishing/ice fishing
boating/canoeing

boat ramp
motor limit: electric only, 12-volt max.
hunting
shooting, archery range
berry, mushroom, nut gathering
hiking

La Salle State Fish & Wildlife Area

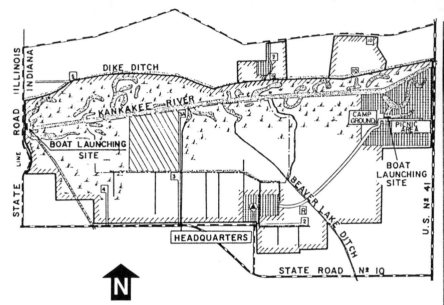

Hiking is another popular activity at the fish and wildlife areas.

For Information

La Salle State Fish & Wildlife Area
R.R. #2, Box 80
Lake Village, IN 46349
(219) 992-3019

Location

La Salle State Fish & Wildlife Area is located south of Cedar Lake and just north of S.R. 10 between U.S. 41 and the Illinois state line. From I-65, take exit 230 and head west on S.R. 10 for 12 miles to the area headquarters. The campground is about 1½ miles northeast of headquarters on an area road or may be reached directly from U.S. 41. About half of the property's 3,643 acres is hardwood forests; the rest of the land is marshland, brush, cropland, and fallow fields. La Salle is bisected by the Kankakee River, which flows through the property for about 4 miles. Several bayous lie adjacent to the river channel. A 600-acre marsh provides excellent waterfowl habitat along the river.

Facilities & Activities

open: 4/1–9/30
19 Class C campsites
    pit toilets
water, picnic tables & grills
shelterhouse
picnicking
fishing, ice fishing (limited)
boating/canoeing (no motor limit)
boat ramps
hunting
shooting, archery range
berry, mushroom, nut gathering
hiking

Mississinewa Lake

Frances Slocum State Recreation Area

Miami State Recreation Area

. . . just viewing the lake!

For Information

Mississinewa Lake
R.R. 1, Box 194
Peru, IN 46970
(317) 473-6528

Location

Mississinewa Lake is located about 7 miles southeast of Peru and about 19 miles northwest of Marion. The lake is accessible from S.R. 19 on the west, S.R. 15 on the east, S.R. 124 on the north, and S.R. 13 that bisects the lake. Frances Slocum and Miami are the two recreation areas that offer camping facilities. Frances Slocum State Recreation Area is located on the north side of the lake near the dam off of County Road 700S; this road crosses the dam and is accessible from S.R. 124 as well as from S.R. 13. Miami State Recreation Area is located on the south side of the lake; travel S.R. 19 south of Peru, turn east on County Road 550S (Old Slocum Trail), then north on County Road 650E. The state office is located at Miami.

Mississinewa Lake, the largest of the upper Wabash River reservoirs, is operated as a unit with the Huntington and Salamonie Lakes to reduce flood stages in the upper Wabash River basins. Located on the Mississinewa River, the lake and environs comprise a total of 14,000 acres. At the summer pool level of 737-foot elevation, water forms a 3,181-acre lake, creating a pool length of 20 miles. The shoreline in several areas features steep limestone cliffs. The northwest side of the lake is densely forested.

Facilities & Activities	Frances Slocum SRA	Miami SRA
Class AA campsites sewage, water hook-ups, electrical outlet modern restrooms & showers		39
Class A campsites electrical outlet modern restrooms & showers		335
Class B campsites (walk-in) modern restrooms & showers		7
Class C campsites pit toilets	46	199
camp reservation system (3 major holidays only)		X
dumping station		X
rally campground (accommodates 50)		X
naturalist services		X
picnicking	X	X
picnic shelter	X	
playground equipment		X
swimming beach		X
bathhouse/concessions		X
hunting, fishing	X	X
boat ramp	X	X
boating/waterskiing	X	X
miles of hiking trails	1.5	4.5

Mounds State Park

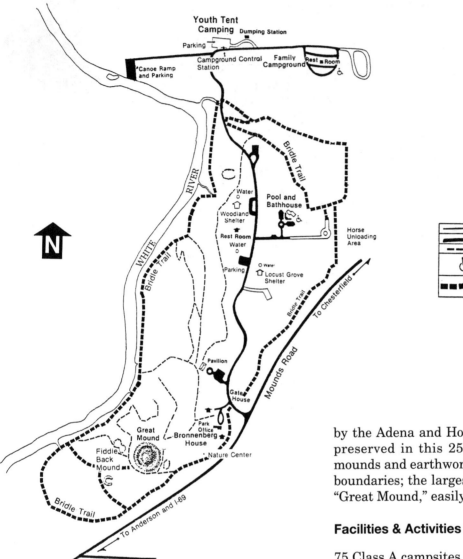

LEGEND

— — —	Park Boundary
▬▬▬	Road
- - - -	Hiking Trail
♿	Usable by Handicapped
■■■■	Bridle and Hiking Trail

by the Adena and Hopewell mound-builders, are preserved in this 259-acre park. There are 11 mounds and earthworks located within the park's boundaries; the largest and best preserved is the "Great Mound," easily accessible by trail.

Facilities & Activities

75 Class A campsites
   electrical outlet
   modern restrooms & showers
campground reservation system
dumping station
camp store
60-site youth tent area
nature center, naturalist services
picnicking, 2 picnic shelters
pavilion (rental 3/1–12/31)
playground equipment
modern swimming pool, bathhouse
concession
fishing
canoe rental, canoe launch on White River
4 hiking trails totaling 4 miles
2½ miles of bridle trails
cross-country skiing, ski rental

For Information

Mounds State Park
4306 Mounds Road
Anderson, IN 46017
(317) 642-6627

Location

Mounds State Park is located off I-69 east of Anderson. From I-69, take the S.R. 32 exit to Chesterfield, then southwest on S.R. 232, also known as Mounds Road. Some of the finest examples of earthwork and mound building in the state, believed to have been constructed about 1–50 A.D.

Ouabache State Park

For Information

Ouabache State Park
6720 E. 100 South
Bluffton, IN 46714
(219) 824-0926

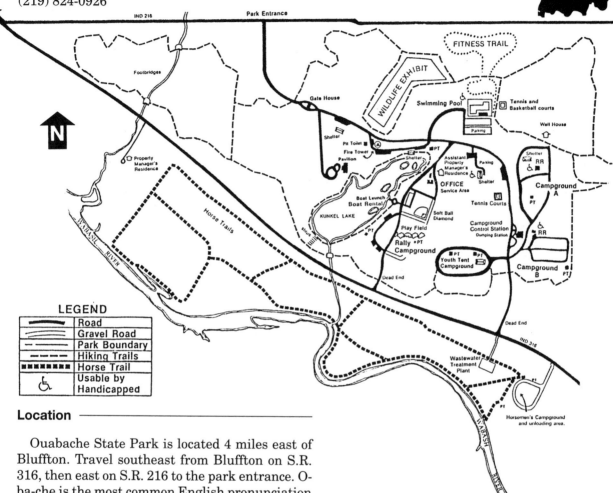

Location

Ouabache State Park is located 4 miles east of Bluffton. Travel southeast from Bluffton on S.R. 316, then east on S.R. 216 to the park entrance. O-ba-che is the most common English pronunciation of this 1,065-acre park. The name "Ouabache" comes from the French Jesuit spelling of the Miami Indian pronunciation of the word, "Wabash." The Wabash River winds along the southern edge of the park.

Facilities & Activities

77 Class A campsites
   electrical outlet
   modern restrooms & showers
47 Class B campsites
   modern restrooms & showers
campground reservation system
dumping station
200-site youth tent area

45-site horsemen's campground
30-site rally campground
wildlife exhibit, naturalist services
picnicking, 4 picnic shelters
lodge (rental 3/1–10/31)
playground equipment
tennis & basketball courts
softball fields
Olympic-size swimming pool, bathhouse
fishing, ice fishing
boating (electric motors only), boat ramp
canoe/rowboat/paddleboat rental
6 hiking trails totaling 13 miles
1-mile fitness trail
bridle trails
cross-country skiing, ski rental

Pigeon River State Fish & Wildlife Area

For Information

Pigeon River State Fish & Wildlife Area
Box 71
Mongo, IN 46771
(219) 367-2164

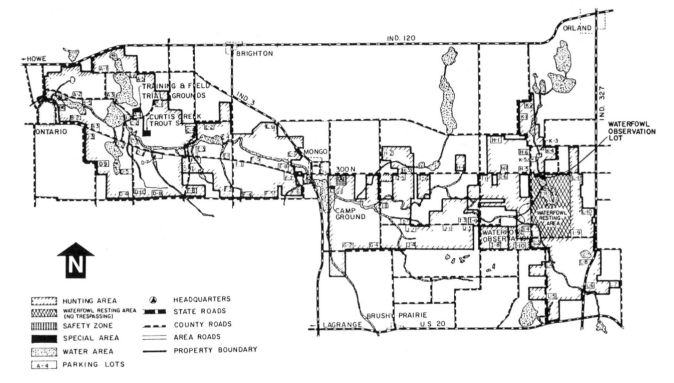

Location

Pigeon River State Fish & Wildlife Area is a long, narrow property that follows the Pigeon River valley. The 11,500-acre property is about 12 miles long and 4 miles wide at its widest point. The river weaves back and forth almost 17 miles within these boundaries. The area headquarters is located on C.R. 300N, which intersects S.R. 3 in the small town of Mongo. The campground is adjacent to headquarters. From I-80/I-90, take exit 120 and travel south on S.R. 9, then east on S.R. 120 to Brighton, then south to Mongo on S.R. 3; or, from I-69, take exit 148 and head west on U.S. 20, then north on S.R. 3. Canoeing the Pigeon River is a popular summer activity—June, July, or August being the best time. The 12-mile portion (from C.R. 900E to S.R. 9) is not difficult to canoe, but there are 3 dams on this section, all of which must be portaged.

Facilities & Activities

44 Class C campsites
   pit toilets
water, picnic tables & grills
picnicking
fishing/ice fishing
water access but no boat ramps
boating/canoeing (motor limit: electric only, 12-volt max on ponds & lakes; unlimited on river and millponds)
boat/canoe rentals (nearby)
hunting
shooting, archery range
berry, mushroom, nut gathering
hiking

Pokagon State Park

Pokagon offers unexcelled recreation for all seasons of the year: lake-oriented in the summer and snow-oriented in the winter.

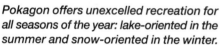

LEGEND

Road	PT	Pit Toilet
Trail	RR	Rest Room
Horse Trail	♿	Usable by
Boundary		Handicapped

For Information

Pokagon State Park
1080 W., State Road 727
Angola, IN 46703
(219) 833-2012 (park)
(219) 833-1077 (inn)

Location

Pokagon State Park is 5 miles north of Angola, borders I-69, and is 1 mile south of I-80/I-90. The Potawatomi Indian tribes ruled for many years in this region. The 1,195-acre park takes its name from one of their famous chiefs, Simon Pokagon; it is located on the shores of Lake James and Snow Lake, amid the rolling hills of Indiana's lake country. Pokagon, a winter wonderland, is the only Indiana State Park with a refrigerated twin toboggan slide.

Facilities & Activities

236 Class A campsites
  electrical outlets
  modern restrooms & showers
99 Class B campsites
  modern restrooms & showers
102 Class C campsites
  pit toilet
campground reservation system
dumping station
camp store, concessions
group camp (capacity: 120 in summer; 40 in winter)
120-site youth tent area
Potawatomi Inn
  meeting & conference facilities
  indoor pool, sauna, jacuzzi
  dining room
  Inn cabins & motel units
nature center, wildlife exhibit, naturalist services
amphitheater
picnicking, 3 picnic shelters
enclosed shelter & warming hut (rental 4/1–10/31)
playground equipment, tennis courts
swimming beach, bathhouse
fishing, ice fishing
motorboating, waterskiing
rowboat/paddleboat rental
6 hiking trails totaling 8 miles
2-mile bridle trail, saddle barn
cross-country skiing, ice skating
1,780-foot twin toboggan slide
sledding

Potato Creek State Park

For Information

Potato Creek State Park
25601 State Road 4
North Liberty, IN 46554
(219) 656-8186

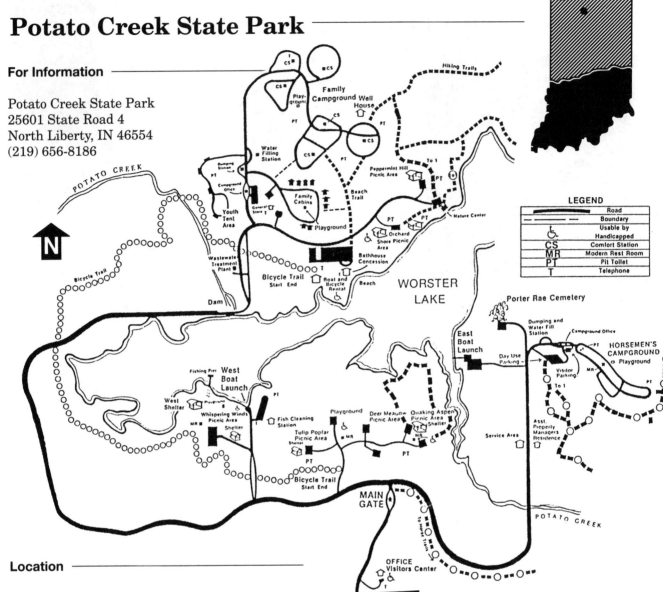

LEGEND

————————	Road
— — — —	Boundary
&#9855;	Usable by Handicapped
CS	Comfort Station
MR	Modern Rest Room
PT	Pit Toilet
T	Telephone

Location

Potato Creek State Park is located 3 miles east of the town of North Liberty on S.R. 4, about 12 miles southwest of Sound Bend, via S.R. 23 or U.S. 31. Worster Lake, the park's 327-acre lake formed by the damming of Potato Creek, has become the main attraction of this 3,840-acre park. However, the park offers a variety of activities for year-round enjoyment.

Facilities & Activities

287-Class A campsites
  electrical outlet
  modern restrooms & showers
campground reservation system
dumping station
camp store, concessions
250-site youth tent area

70-site horsemen's campground
17 family housekeeping cabins (each sleeps 8)
nature center, naturalist services
picnicking, 5 picnic shelters
2 enclosed shelters (rental 4/1–10/31)
playground equipment
swimming beach, bathhouse
fishing, ice fishing, fishing pier
boating (electric motors only), boat ramp
canoe/rowboat/paddleboat rental
3.2-mile bicycle trail, bicycle rental
4 hiking trails totaling 6 miles
2 bridle trails totaling 8 miles
8 miles of cross-country ski trails, ski rental
ice skating
tubing/sledding

Raccoon State Recreation Area/ Cecil M. Harden Lake

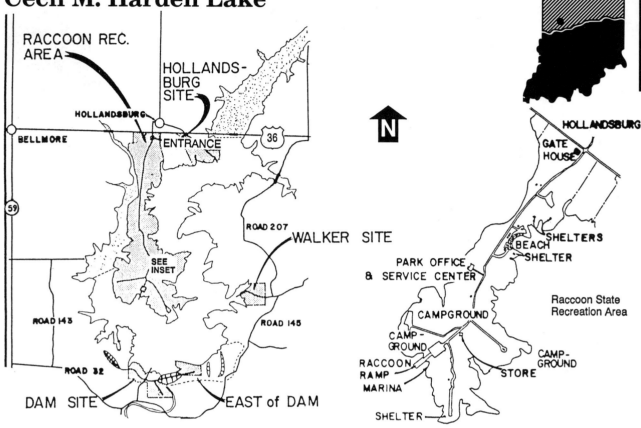

For Information

Raccoon State Recreation Area
R.R. 1, Box 59
Rockville, IN 47872
(317) 344-1412 (office)
(317) 344-1884 (reservations)

Location

Cecil M. Harden Lake is about 50 miles west of Indianapolis and 25 miles northeast of Terre Haute. The lake is accessible from U.S. 36 and secondary roads leading from S.R. 59. This reservoir is known by 2 names: Cecil M. Harden Lake and Raccoon State Recreation Area. The entrance to Raccoon State Recreation Area is from U.S. 36; the park office is located on the property.

Cecil M. Harden Lake is operated primarily for flood control in the Raccoon Creek and Wabash River watersheds. The lake comprises 4,065 acres; at the summer pool level of 661-foot elevation, 2,060 acres of water form the lake and create a pool length of 10.3 miles. The lake shoreline is moderately steep and dominated by native trees of tulip poplar, white oak, sugar maple, sassafras, and ash. In the fall, the foliage of these trees adds significantly to the beauty of the lake.

Facilities & Activities

236 Class A campsites
    electrical outlets
    modern restrooms & showers
56 Class B campsites
    modern restrooms & showers
50 Class C campsites
    pit toilets
camp reservation system
dumping station
camp store, concessions
naturalist services
picnicking, picnic shelters
playground equipment
swimming beach, bathhouse
hunting, fishing, ice fishing (limited)
marina/boat rental
boating/waterskiing/4 boat ramps
4½ miles of hiking trails
cross-country skiing

Salamonie Lake

Lost Bridge East/West State Recreation Areas

Mount Etna State Recreation Area

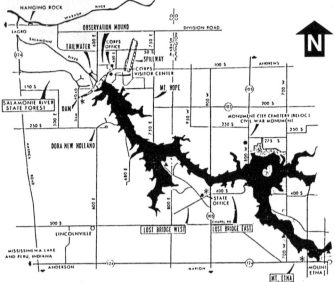

The only marina at Salamonie Lake is at Lost Bridge West State Recreation Area.

For Information

Salamonie Lake
9214 West-Lost Bridge West
Andrews, IN 46702
(219) 468-2125

Location

Salamonie Lake is located between Wabash and Huntington south of U.S. 24 and accessible from S.R. 524, 105, 9, and 124. The lake has 3 recreation areas that offer camping facilities: Lost Bridge West, Lost Bridge East, and Mount Etna. Lost Bridge West State Recreation Area has the most developed campground; Lost Bridge East SRA and Mount Etna SRA are both primitive campgrounds. All 3 recreation areas are on the south side of the lake. Lost Bridge West is west of S.R. 105 on C.R. 400S and Lost Bridge East is east of S.R. 105 on C.R. 400S. The property office is located at Lost Bridge West. Mt. Etna is just north of S.R. 124 on C.R. 700W.

Salamonie Lake is one of the three "sister" lakes and is the second largest reservoir of the Upper Wabash River Basin project. Located on the Salamonie River, the dam is 3.1 miles above where its mouth enters the Wabash River. Salamonie Lake and environs comprise 11,506 acres. At the summer pool level of 755 foot elevation, water forms a 2,855-acre lake and creates a pool length of 17 miles. Salamonie River State Forest lies just below the dam and is the only state forest left in northern Indiana.

Facilities & Activities

	Lost Bridge East SRA	Lost Bridge West SRA	Mount Etna SRA
Class A campsites electrical outlet modern restrooms & showers		240	
Class C campsites (180) pit toilets	X	X	X
camp reservation system (3 major holidays only)		X	
dumping station		X	
youth group campground (60)	X		
horsemen's campsites (45)		X	
naturalist services		X	
picnicking	X	X	X
picnic shelter	X		
playground equipment	X	X	
swimming beach, bathhouse/concessions		X	
hunting, fishing	X	X	X
marina/boat rental/supplies		X	
boating/waterskiing/boat ramp	X	X	X
miles of hiking trails		2.5	
(6-mile Lakeview Trail connects * with *)	X*		X*
miles of bridle trails (plus 19 miles in state forest)		9	
cross-country ski trails	X	X	X
snowmobile trail	X		X

Salamonie River State Forest

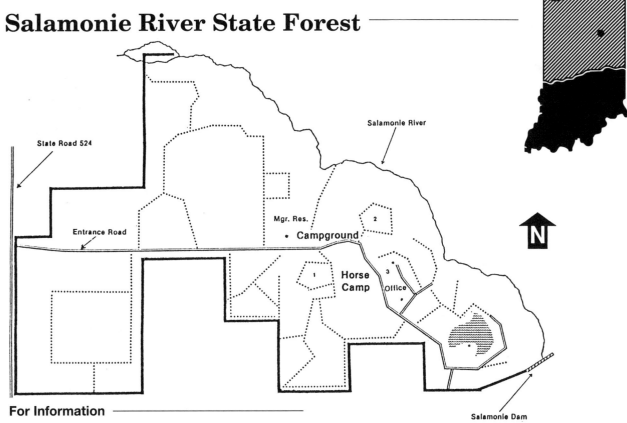

For Information

Salamonie River State Forest
R.R. 1, Box 89
Lagro, IN 46941
(219) 782-2349

Location

Salamonie River State Forest is located about 8 miles east of Wabash, and is accessible from S.R. 254 south from U.S. 24 at the town of Lagro. The Salamonie River, downstream from the Salamonie Dam is the northeast boundary for this 621-acre property. The forest has a large network of trails for hiking, horseback riding, and cross-country skiing, while the 11-acre Hominy Ridge Lake provides good fishing. Two separate campgrounds are provided for family camping.

Facilities & Activities

32 Class C campsites (2 locations)
   pit toilets
dumping station
4 youth tent areas
10-site horsemen's camp
picnicking, picnic shelters
playground equipment
hunting, fishing, ice fishing
boating (electric motors only), boat ramp
9 miles of hiking trails
19 miles of bridle trails
9 miles of cross-country ski trails

The state forest at Salamonie River has 9 miles of cross-country ski trails.

Shades State Park

For Information

Shades State Park
Route 1, Box 72
Waveland, IN 47989
(317) 435-2810

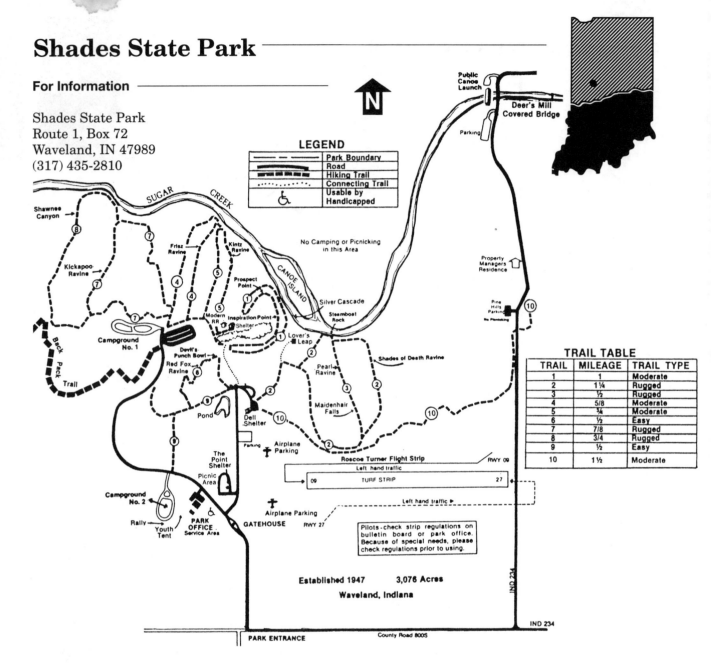

LEGEND

	Park Boundary
	Road
	Hiking Trail
	Connecting Trail
♿	Usable by Handicapped

No Camping or Picnicking in this Area

Pilots - check strip regulations on bulletin board or park office. Because of special needs, please check regulations prior to using.

Established 1947   3,076 Acres

Waveland, Indiana

TRAIL TABLE

TRAIL	MILEAGE	TRAIL TYPE
1	1	Moderate
2	1¼	Rugged
3	½	Rugged
4	5/8	Moderate
5	¾	Moderate
6	½	Easy
7	7/8	Rugged
8	3/4	Rugged
9	½	Easy
10	1½	Moderate

Location

Shades State Park is located southwest of Crawfordsville and south of I-74, between U.S. 41 and U.S. 231. The park entrance is on S.R. 234. This 3,076-acre park is maintained as a more natural park with less modern development to protect its natural and fragile areas. Shades is the only park that provides canoe camping and backpack camping. Beautiful sandstone cliffs overlook Sugar Creek, one of the most canoed creeks in the state.

Facilities & Activities

105 Class B campsites
   modern restrooms & showers
NO campground reservation system
dumping station
220-site youth tent area
30-site rally campground
backpack campground
canoe campground
naturalist services
picnicking, 3 picnic shelters
playground equipment
fishing
canoe launch & rental at Deer's Mill Covered
   Bridge
bicycle rental
11 hiking trails totaling 15 miles
3000′ × 120′ flight strip, E-W turf for light aircraft

Summit Lake State Park

For Information

Summit Lake State Park
Route 4, Box 33C
New Castle, IN 47362
(317) 766-5873

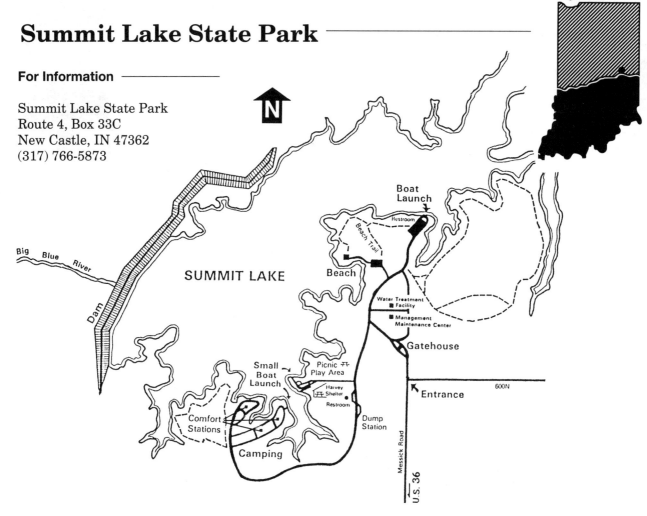

N

Boat Launch

Restroom

Beach Trail

Beach

Big Blue River

Dam

SUMMIT LAKE

Water Treatment Facility

Management Maintenance Center

Gatehouse

Small Boat Launch

Picnic Play Area

Harvey Shelter

Restroom

Comfort Stations

Camping

Dump Station

Entrance

600N

Messick Road

U.S. 36

Location

Summit Lake State Park is located south of Muncie and 8 miles northeast of New Castle; from Mount Summit, on S.R. 3, travel east on U.S. 36 to Messick Road, then north to the park entrance. On January 9, 1988, Summit Lake became the newest state park in Indiana. The 2,552-acres includes a 500-acre lake, shady wooded areas, and lots of open space. The interpretive center is a reconstruction of the home in which aviation pioneer Wilbur Wright was born; it houses a display about the Wright Brothers and early aviation, as well as some nature exhibits.

Facilities & Activities

125 Class A campsites
   electrical outlet
   modern restrooms & showers
NO campground reservation system
dumping station
interpretative center, naturalist services
picnicking, 1 picnic shelter
playground equipment
swimming beach, bathhouse, concessions
fishing, ice fishing
motorboating (operate at idle speed only)
3 boat ramps
canoe/rowboat/paddleboat rental
bicycle rental
3 hiking trails totaling 3¾ miles
cross-country skiing

Don't you know these youngsters are glad this park rents bicycles?

Tippecanoe River State Park

For Information

Tippecanoe River State Park
Route 4, Box 95A
Winamac, IN 46996
(219) 946-3213

LEGEND

— — —	Park Boundary
▬▬▬	Roads: TR1, TR2
≈≈≈≈	Gravel Road
▪▪▪▪	Hiking Trail
••••••	Horse Trail
RR	Restroom
♿	Usable by Handicapped
– — –	Abandoned Railroad Bed

ROADS

TR1	3½ mile paved loop from gate
TR2	2 mile paved/gravel road N/S

Location

Tippecanoe River State Park is located approximately midway between Logansport and La Porte, with access from U.S. 35. The 2,761-acre park is located on the east side of U.S. 35 while Winamac Fish and Wildlife Area is located just west of the highway. The Tippecanoe River, a popular river to canoe, meanders approximately 7 miles along the eastern border of the park.

Facilities & Activities

112 Class A campsites
    electrical outlet
    modern restrooms & showers
NO campground reservation system
dumping station
group camp with kitchen (160 capacity)
youth tent area (120 capacity)
60-site horsemen's campground
10-site canoe campground (with launch)
12 rent-a-tents
naturalist services
picnicking, 2 picnic shelters
recreation building (rental 3/1–10/30)
playground equipment
fishing, boat launch
bicycle rental
10 miles of hiking trails
12½ miles of bridle trails
cross-country skiing, ski rental

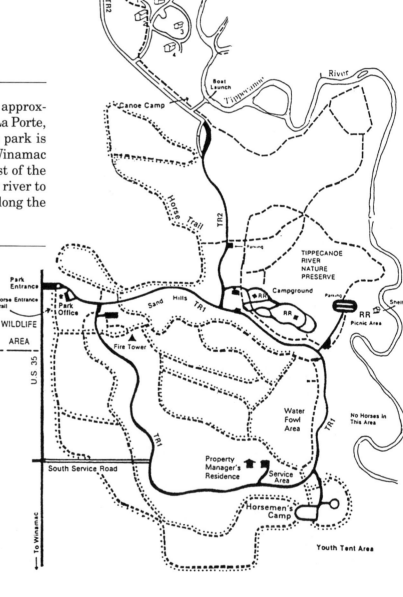

Turkey Run State Park

For Information

Turkey Run State Park
Route 1, Box 164
Marshall, IN 47859
(317) 597-2635 (park)
(317) 597-2211 (inn)

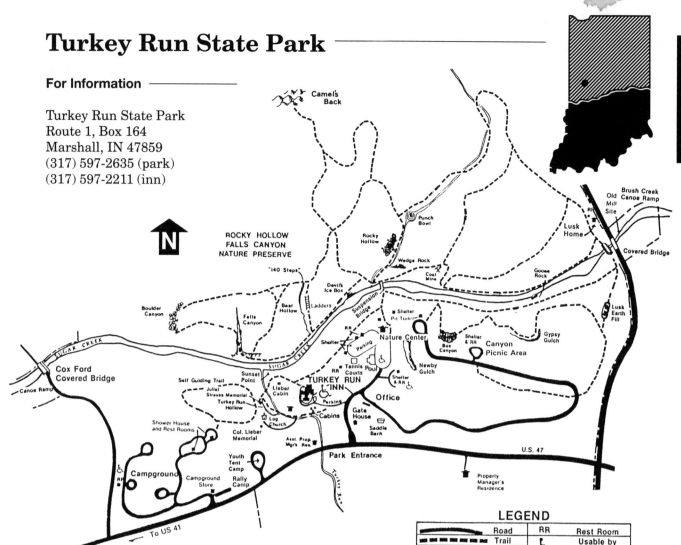

Location

Turkey Run State Park is located on S.R. 47, just 2 miles east of the junction of U.S. 41 and S.R. 47. The entrance to the campground is separate from the park's main entrance; however, both are off of S.R. 47. The main natural attractions at this 2,382-acre park are hiking in the Rocky Hollow Falls Canyon Nature Preserve and canoeing on Sugar Creek. Deep sandstone ravines have been carved in the Sugar Creek stream bed as well as many of the canyons of Turkey Run.

Facilities & Activities

235 Class A campsites
   electrical outlets
   modern restrooms & showers
29 Class B campsites
   modern restrooms & showers
campground reservation system
dumping station
camp store
60-site youth tent area
15-site rally campground
52-room Turkey Run Inn
   meeting & conference facilities
   dining room
   21 Inn cabins
nature center, naturalist sevices
picnicking, 6 picnic shelters
playground equipment
tennis courts
Olympic-size swimming pool
bathhouse
fishing
canoe ramps
canoe rentals (nearby)
bicycle rental
10 hiking trails totaling 14 miles
bridle trails, saddle barn
horse rental

Willow Slough State Fish & Wildlife Area

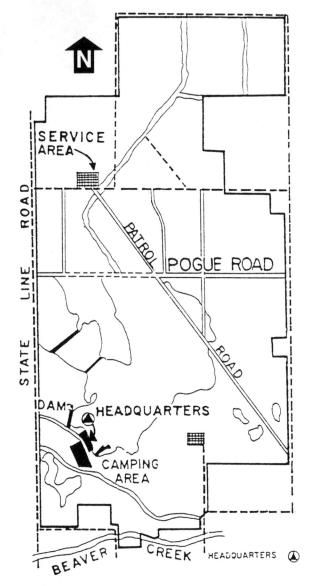

For Information

Willow Slough State Fish &
  Wildlife Area
R.R. #2
Morocco, IN 47963
(219) 285-2704

Location

Willow Slough State Fish & Wildlife Area is located on the Illinois border west of U.S. 41, north of S.R. 114, and northwest of the small town of Morocco. From U.S. 41, just north of Morocco, take County Road 275S to area headquarters. The camping area is near the park headquarters on the south edge of Murphey Lake. The property comprises 9,640 acres, including about 2,300 acres of open water and marshes and flooded cropland. This area attracts large numbers of ice fishermen and waterfowlers to the 1,300-acre Murphey Lake. The area is diverse, consisting of high, sandy hills and oak barrens, poorly drained lowlands, farmland, and lakes and marshes.

Facilities & Activities

74 Class B campsites
  modern restrooms & showers
  (showerhouse closed in winter)
water, picnic tables & grills
dumping station
shelterhouse
picnicking
fishing/ice fishing
boat launching ramp
boating/canoeing
  motor limit: electric only, 12-volt max.
boat/canoe rentals
hunting
shooting, archery range
berry, mushroom, nut gathering
hiking

In season, many ice fishermen are attracted to these same waters.

Indiana
Region 2 ———————

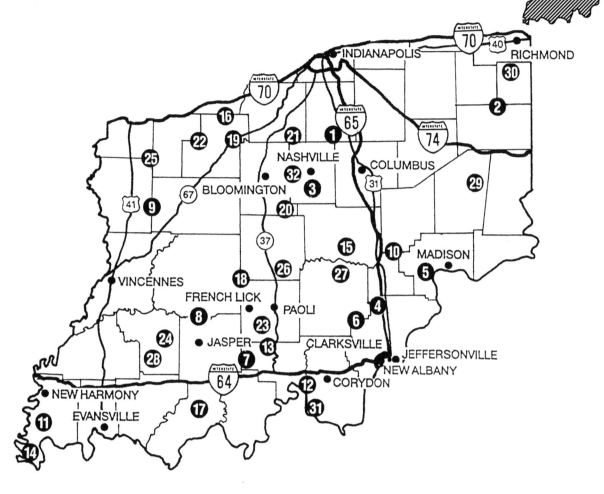

Atterbury State Fish & Wildlife Area

For Information

Atterbury State Fish & Wildlife Area
Edinburg, IN 46124
(812) 526-2051

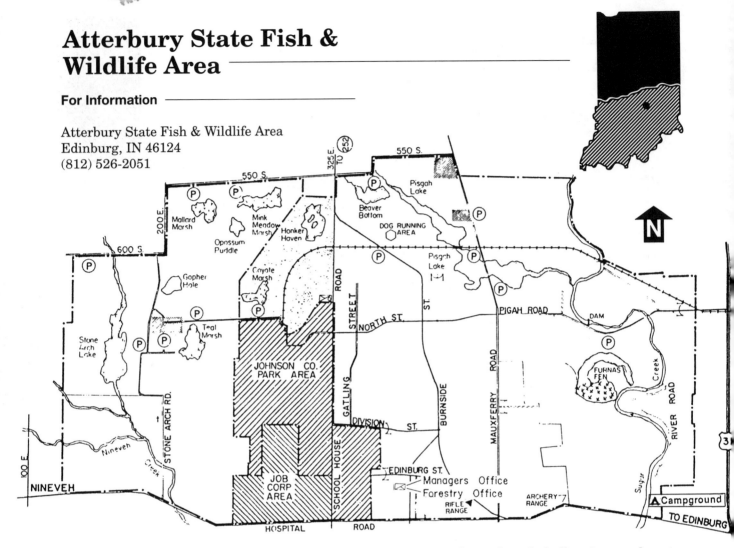

Location

Atterbury State Fish & Wildlife Area is located 30 miles south of Indianapolis, via exit 80 on I-65. Head west on S.R. 252, cross U.S. 31 and continue on Hospital Road. The campground is on River Road in the southeast corner of the 5,512-acre property. The acreage is upland game habitat and 200 acres of marsh and shallow impoundments. Atterbury is part of an old World War II infantry camp called Camp Atterbury. There are 10 man-made impoundments, ranging from 1 to 65 acres in size. The topography is flat to gently rolling, with a few deep ravines along Sugar Creek.

Facilities & Activities

30 Class C campsites
   pit toilets
water, picnic tables & grills
picnicking
fishing/ice fishing
special fishing pier for handicapped fishermen at
   Beaver Bottom Pond
boating/canoeing
boat ramps
   motor limit: electric only, 12-volt max.
hunting
shooting, archery range
berry, mushroom, nut gathering
hiking

This photographer certainly takes her work seriously!

Brookville Lake
Mounds State Recreation Area
Quakertown State Recreation Area

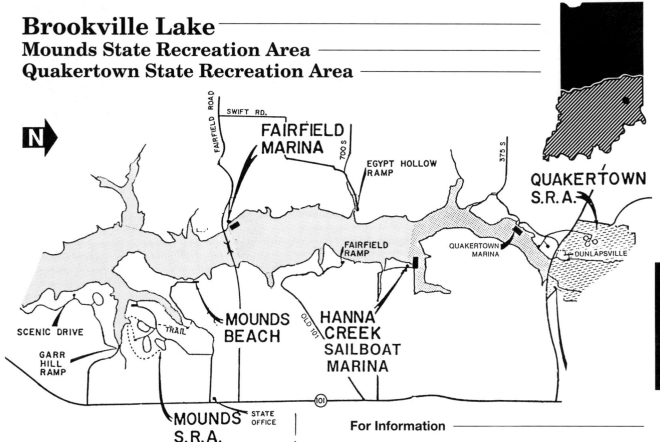

Facilities & Activities

	Mounds SRA	Quakertown SRA
Class AA campsites sewage, water hook-ups, electrical outlet modern restrooms & showers	57	
Class A campsites electrical outlet modern restrooms & showers	275	97
camp reservation system	X	
dumping station	X	X
camp store	X	
naturalist services	X	X
picnicking, picnic shelters	X	X
playground equipment	X	X
swimming beach	X	X
bathhouse/concessions	X	X
hunting, fishing/ ice fishing	X	X
fish cleaning station	X	
marina/boat rental		X
boating/waterskiing	X	X
boat ramp	X	X
hiking trails	X	X

For Information

Brookville Lake
P.O. Box 100
Brookville, IN 47012
(317) 647-6557

Location

Brookville Lake is southeast of Connersville and accessible from S.R. 101 on the east and S.R. 1 on the west. These 2 state roads converge near U.S. 52 in Brookville, just 1½ miles below the dam and spillway. Brookville Lake has 2 major recreation areas: Mounds and Quakertown. Access to Mounds State Recreation Area is from S.R. 101; the reservoir office is located here. Quakertown State Recreation Area is accessible from either S.R. 1 or S.R. 101 via Roseburg Road (75 S); this road divides the campground area from the beach and marina area.

Brookville Lake, located on the east fork of the Whitewater River, is operated for flood control in the Whitewater Valley. The lake and surrounding land comprise a total of 16,445 acres; at the summer pool level of 748-foot elevation, 5,260 acres of water form the lake and create a pool length of 16.4 miles. In the heart of the Whitewater River Valley, this area has long been acknowledged as one of the most picturesque in the state.

Brown County State Park

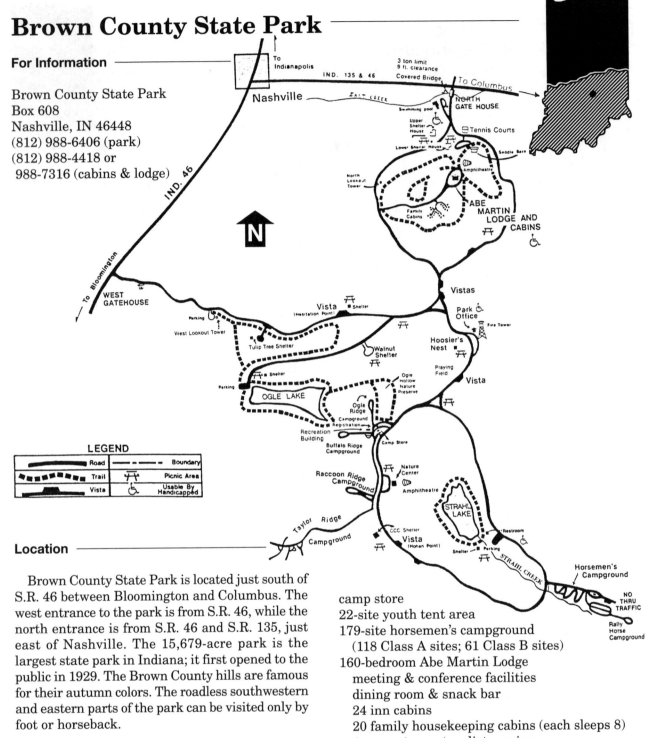

LEGEND

▬▬▬ Road	– – – Boundary
■-■-■ Trail	⛢ Picnic Area
▬ Vista	♿ Usable By Handicapped

Location

Brown County State Park is located just south of S.R. 46 between Bloomington and Columbus. The west entrance to the park is from S.R. 46, while the north entrance is from S.R. 46 and S.R. 135, just east of Nashville. The 15,679-acre park is the largest state park in Indiana; it first opened to the public in 1929. The Brown County hills are famous for their autumn colors. The roadless southwestern and eastern parts of the park can be visited only by foot or horseback.

Facilities & Activities

401 Class A campsites
  electrical outlet
  modern restrooms & showers
28 Class B campsites
  modern restrooms & showers
campground reservation system
dumping station
camp store
22-site youth tent area
179-site horsemen's campground
  (118 Class A sites; 61 Class B sites)
160-bedroom Abe Martin Lodge
  meeting & conference facilities
  dining room & snack bar
  24 inn cabins
  20 family housekeeping cabins (each sleeps 8)
nature center, naturalist services
picnicking, 9 picnic shelters
recreation building (rental 3/1–10/31)
playground equipment
tennis courts
Olympic-size swimming pool
fishing, ice fishing
12 miles of hiking trails
49 miles bridle trails, saddle barn
cross-country skiing

Clark State Forest

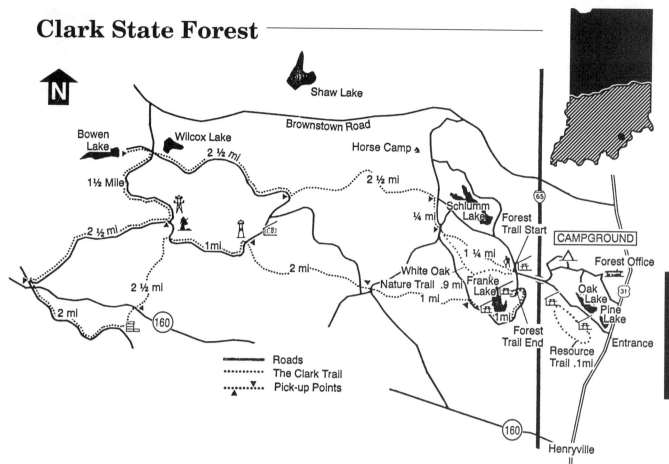

Roads ━━━
The Clark Trail ·········
Pick-up Points ·····▼·····▲

Location

Clark State Forest is located just west of U.S. 31/I-65 between Scottsburg and New Albany. The entrance to the forest office, as well as to the campground is 1 mile north of Henryville on U.S. 31; if traveling on I-65, take the Henryville exit. This 23,979-acre state forest is the oldest in Indiana; it was established in 1903. Beautiful roads and trails wind through the heavily forested timberland. There are 6 fine fishing lakes ranging in size from 2 to 18 acres.

Facilities & Activities

70 Class C campsites
  pit toilets
dumping station
group camping
10-site horsemen's camp
backpack camping
picnicking, 7 picnic shelters
playground equipment
hunting, fishing, ice fishing
boating (electric motors only)
boat ramp
4 hiking trails totaling 80 miles (includes portion of Knobstone Trail)
100 miles of bridle trails

For Information

Clark State Forest
P.O. Box 119
Henryville, IN 47126
(812) 294-4306

Fun for this family includes wading the stream.

Clifty Falls State Park

For Information

Clifty Falls State Park
1501 Green Road
Madison, IN 47250
(812) 265-1331 (park)
(812) 265-4135 (inn)

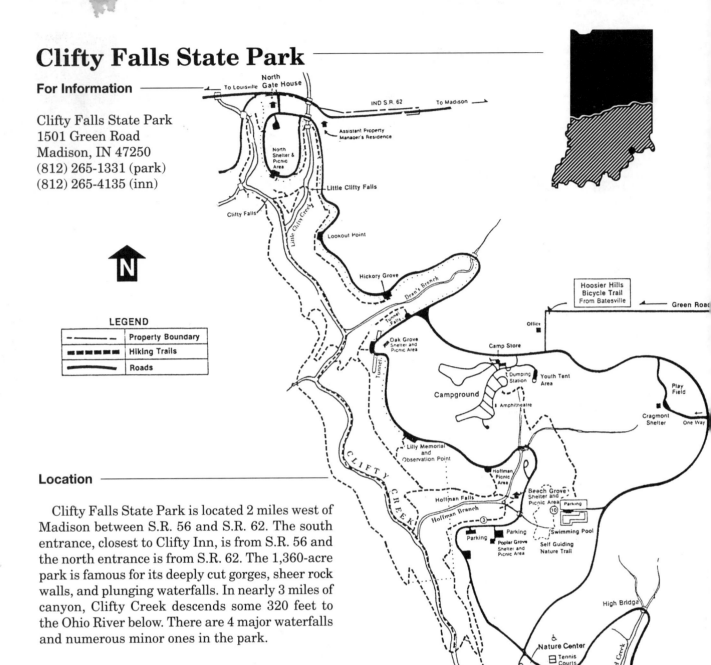

LEGEND

– – – –	Property Boundary
■■■■■	Hiking Trails
——	Roads

Location

Clifty Falls State Park is located 2 miles west of Madison between S.R. 56 and S.R. 62. The south entrance, closest to Clifty Inn, is from S.R. 56 and the north entrance is from S.R. 62. The 1,360-acre park is famous for its deeply cut gorges, sheer rock walls, and plunging waterfalls. In nearly 3 miles of canyon, Clifty Creek descends some 320 feet to the Ohio River below. There are 4 major waterfalls and numerous minor ones in the park.

Facilities & Activities

106 Class A campsites
    electrical outlets
    modern restrooms & showers
59 Class C campsites
    pit toilets
campground reservation system
dumping station
150-site youth tent area
72-room Clifty Inn
    meeting & conference facilities
    dining room
nature center, naturalist services
picnicking, 5 picnic shelters
playground equipment

tennis courts
Olympic-size swimming pool, bathhouse
water slide
12 miles of hiking trails

Deam Lake State Recreation Area

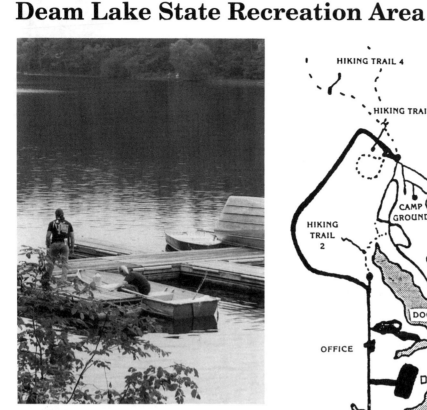

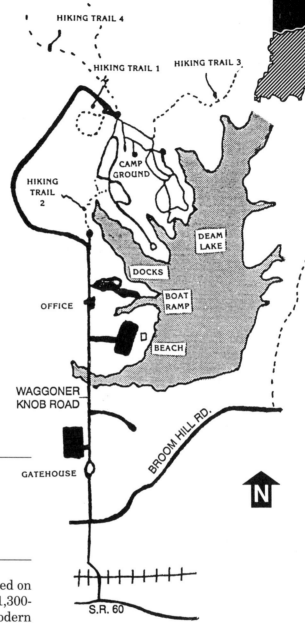

Rowboat rental is popular at Deam Lake because boating is limited to electric motors only.

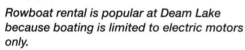

For Information

Deam Lake State Recreation Area
1217 Deam Lake Road
Borden, IN 47106
(812) 246-5421

Location

Deam Lake State Recreation Area is located on the southern edge of Clark State Forest. The 1,300-acre recreation area has one of the two modern campgrounds in the state forest system. From I-65, north of Louisville, take the S.R. 60 exit and travel northwest toward Salem. The recreation area is 8 miles north of Hamburg and 6 miles south of New Providence. The 194-acre Deam Lake is the center of attraction; the swimming beach is open from Memorial Day through Labor Day. The campground is closed from November through February.

Facilities & Activities

280 Class A campsites
   electrical outlet
   modern restrooms & showers
campground reservation system
   (Memorial weekend–Labor Day)
dumping station
camp store, snack bar
picnicking, picnic shelters
playground equipment
swimming beach, bathhouse
hunting, fishing, ice fishing
boating (electric motors only)
boat ramp
sailing/windsurfing
rowboat rental
4 hiking trails

Ferdinand State Forest

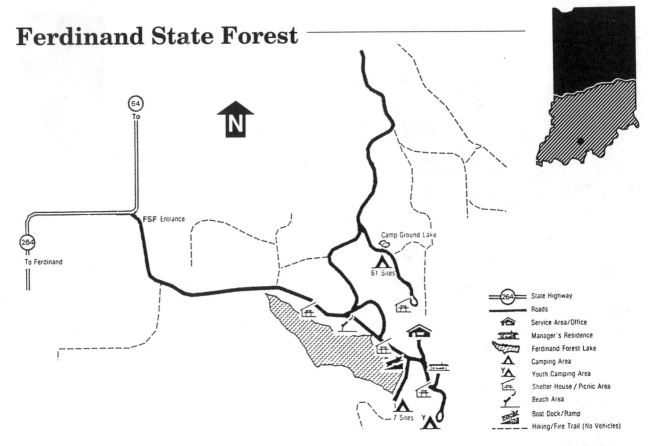

![264]	State Highway
	Roads
	Service Area/Office
	Manager's Residence
	Ferdinand Forest Lake
	Camping Area
	Youth Camping Area
	Shelter House / Picnic Area
	Beach Area
	Boat Dock/Ramp
- - - -	Hiking/Fire Trail (No Vehicles)

For Information

Ferdinand State Forest
6583 E. State Road 264
Ferdinand, IN 47532
(812) 367-1524

Location

Ferdinand State Forest is located north of I-64 and southeast of Jasper. From I-64, take exit 63 and travel north on S.R. 162 through the small town of Ferdinand. The forest entrance is 6 miles east of Ferdinand on S.R. 264. The 7,657-acre forest has a 42-acre lake, acclaimed to be one of the most beautiful forest lakes in the state. This area is rich in German heritage with many local landmarks and seasonal community festivals.

Ferdinand State Forest is acclaimed to be one of the most beautiful forest lakes in the state.

Facilities & Activities

72 Class C campsites
   pit toilets
dumping station
youth tent area
picnicking, picnic shelters
playground equipment

swimming beach
hunting, fishing, ice fishing
boating (electric motors only)
boat ramp
rowboat rental
hiking trails

Glendale State Fish & Wildlife Area

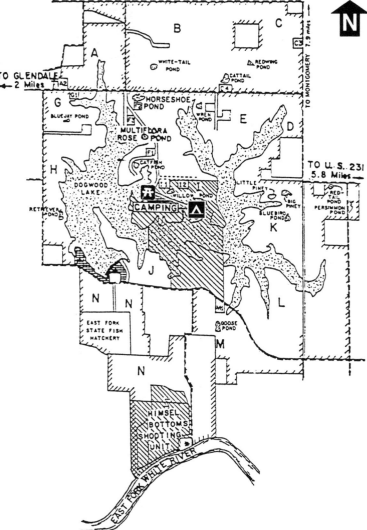

. . . a rare opportunity for father and son to spend some "quality time" together.

The average depth of Dogwood Lake is 8 feet. The land ranges from level to steep sloping hills; about one-fourth of the land is forest, the rest is brush and fields. Of the 9 state fish and wildlife areas that provide camping facilities, Glendale has the only campsites with electricity.

Facilities & Activities

67 Class A campsites
  electrical outlets
  modern restrooms & showers
50 Class B campsites
  modern restrooms & showers
(comfort station open 4/1–10/31)
water, picnic tables & grills
picnicking
fishing, ice fishing
boating/canoeing
boat ramps
motor limit: 10 h.p.
boat/canoe rental
hunting
archery range
berry, mushroom, nut gathering
hiking

For Information

Glendale State Fish & Wildlife Area
R.R. #2, Box 300
Montgomery, IN 47558
(812) 644-7711

Location

Glendale State Fish & Wildlife Area is located 7 miles southeast of Washington via S.R. 257; turn east to Glendale and follow signs to headquarters. The campground is less than ½-mile beyond headquarters. This 8,020-acre property includes the 1,400-acre Dogwood Lake and several small ponds.

INDIANA REGION 2

Greene-Sullivan State Forest

For Information

Greene-Sullivan State Forest
R.R. 1, Box 382
Dugger, IN 47848
(812) 648-2810

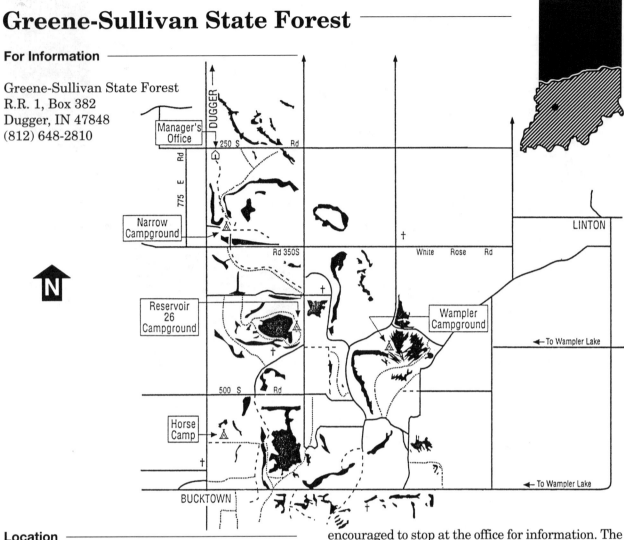

Location

Greene-Sullivan State Forest is located east of S.R. 159 between Dugger and Pleasantville. When traveling south from Dugger, the forest manager's office is on the left at the intersection of S.R. 159 and County Road 250S. First-time visitors are encouraged to stop at the office for information. The county roads within the forest are paved, but many of the property roads are gravel. There are 3 primitive campgrounds plus the equestrian camp; Reservoir 26 is the main campground. The forest is composed of 6,764 acres of reclaimed surface mined lands and contains more than 100 fishing lakes.

This tent is quite roomy and quite ideal for enjoying the primitive setting at a state forest.

Facilities & Activities

130 Class C campsites (pit toilets)
   50 at Reservoir 26
   50 at Wampler
   30 at Narrow
dumping station
20-site equestrian campground
picnicking, picnic shelters
playground equipment
hunting, fishing, ice fishing
boating (electric motors only)
boat ramps
hiking trails
25 miles of bridle trails

Hardy Lake State Recreation Area

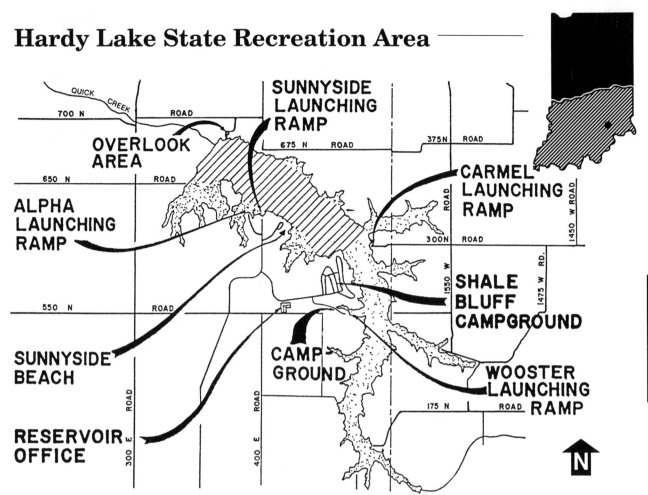

For Information

Hardy Lake
R.R. 4, Box 174
Scottsburg, IN 47170
(812) 794-3800

Location

Hardy Lake is 8 miles northeast of Austin and accessible from S.R. 256 between Austin and Madison. From S.R. 256, travel north on S.R. 203 to reach Hardy State Recreation Area. As you approach the recreation area, the beach, marina, and 2 of the boat ramps are to the left; the reservoir office and 2 campgrounds are to the right. Wooster Campground, designed primarily to serve fishermen and primitive campers, also has a boat ramp.

Hardy Lake is the smallest reservoir of the 9 multi-use recreation areas managed by the Division of Reservoir Management. The lake's total acreage consists of 2,062 acres with a water surface area of 741 acres. Unlike most reservoirs, a stable pool elevation of 600 feet is maintained throughout the year and seldom fluctuates more than 1 foot. At normal pool, there are 3.4 miles of backwater and a depth of 37 feet at the dam.

Facilities & Activities

149 Class A campsites (Shale Bluff Campground)
   electrical outlet
     modern restrooms & showers
     dumping station
19 Class C campsites (Wooster Campground)
   pit toilets
camp reservation system
naturalist services
picnicking, picnic shelters
playground equipment
swimming beach
bathhouse/concessions
hunting, fishing, ice fishing
2 fishing piers
marina/boat rental
boating/water skiing
4 boat ramps
6 miles of hiking trails

Harmonie State Park

For Information

Harmonie State Park
Route 1, Box 5A
New Harmony, IN 47631
(812) 682-4821

LEGEND	
▄▄▄▄	Hiking Trail
— —	Park Boundary
PT	Pit Toilet
RR	Rest Room
♿	Usable by Handicapped
—··—··—	Horse Trail

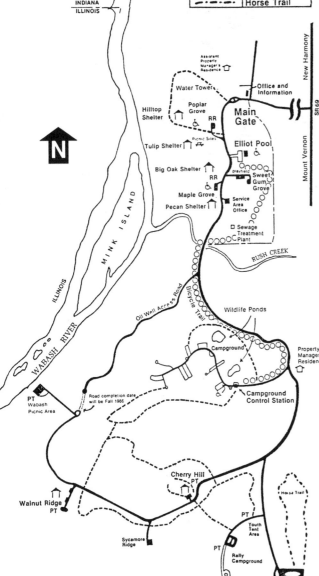

S.R. 69 north to the park entrance. From I-64, take exit 12 at Poseyville and head southwest on S.R. 68 to New Harmony. The topography of the 3,465-acre park varies from flat flood plains along the Wabash River to rolling hills in the camping areas.

Facilities & Activities

199 Class A campsites
  electrical outlet
  modern restrooms & showers
NO campground reservation system
dumping station
camp store
90-site youth tent area
150-site rally campground
11 family housekeeping cabins (2 sleep 6; 9 sleep 8)
nature center, naturalist services
picnicking, 6 picnic shelters
playground equipment
Olympic-size swimming pool
bathhouse
110-foot water slide
fishing
boat ramp (into Wabash River)
bicycle rental
3 miles of bicycle trails
8 miles of hiking trails
3½ miles of bridle trails

"Look how high I can climb!"

Location

Harmonie State Park is located "on the banks of the Wabash," approximately 25 miles northwest of Evansville, via S.R. 66 to New Harmony, then 4 miles south on S.R. 69. From Mt. Vernon, take

Harrison-Crawford State Forest

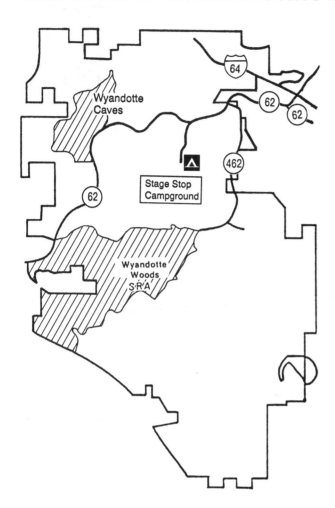

For Information

Harrison-Crawford State Forest
7240 Old Forest Road
Corydon, IN 47112
(812) 738-8232

Location

Harrison-Crawford State Forest lies in the central and extreme southern part of the state and borders the Ohio River. Entrance to the forest is via S.R. 62. From I-64, west of the forest, take exit 92 (Leavenworth, S.R. 66); travel south on S.R. 66, then east on S.R. 62. From I-64, east of the forest, take exit 105 (Corydon, S.R. 135); travel south on S.R. 135, then west on S.R. 62. The entrance to Stage Stop Campground, located along Blue River, is on S.R. 62. The 25,619-acre forest includes the Wyandotte Woods State Recreation Area and the Wyandotte Caves State Recreation Area. Wyandotte Woods SRA offers Class A campsites; Wyandotte Caves SRA offers tours through both Little and Big Wyandotte Caves, but does not offer camping. This large forest has plenty to offer the camper, backpacker, and river enthusiast.

Facilities & Activities

60 Class C campsites (Stage Stop Campground)
   pit toilets
youth group tent area
backpack camping
canoe camping
picnicking, 4 picnic shelters
hunting, fishing, ice fishing
archery range
canoe access ramp (at Stage Stop on Blue River)
canoeing/tubing (on Blue River)
canoe rental (available nearby)
10 hiking trails totaling 42 miles
100 miles of bridle trails

Stage Stop Campground is popular with canoe campers; it has a canoe access ramp to the Blue River.

Hoosier National Forest

For Information

Forest Supervisor
Wayne-Hoosier National Forest
811 Constitution Avenue
Bedford, IN 47421
(812) 275-5987

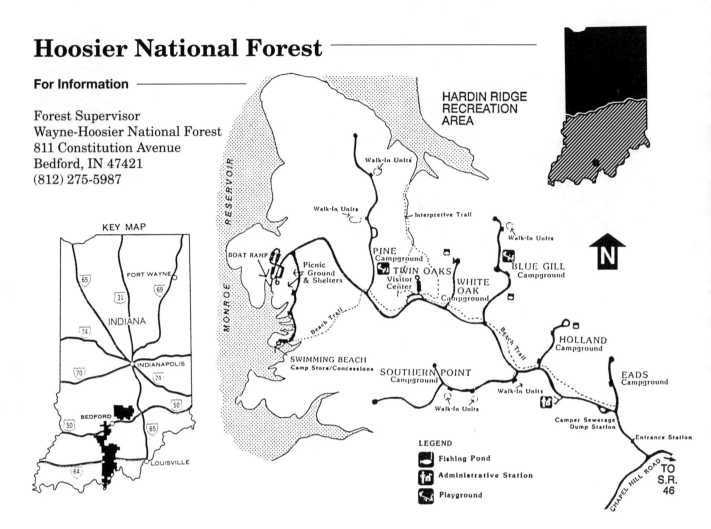

KEY MAP

HARDIN RIDGE RECREATION AREA

LEGEND
- Fishing Pond
- Administrative Station
- Playground

About the Forest

The Hoosier National Forest, established in 1951, is located in the rolling hills of southern Indiana; to the south, it is backed against the Ohio River. A principal access route from Indianapolis is S.R. 37. The exterior boundaries of the forest contain 430,000 acres; the national forest lands within that boundary now total almost 188,000 acres. There are two ranger districts: Brownstown and Tell City. For administration, the Hoosier is linked with the Wayne National Forest in Ohio.

Materials on recreational opportunities on the Hoosier National Forest are available from the two district ranger offices as well as from the office of the forest supervisor. All national forest lands are available for primitive camping, hiking, fishing, and hunting; contact them for maps and specific information. They also have information on such items as winter activities, hiking, horse trails, and opening and closing dates for campgrounds.

Facilities on the Hoosier National Forest include 7 campgrounds, with 365 units, 1 group camp, 6 picnic areas, 4 swimming beaches, 7 boat ramps, 24 miles of hiking trails, 4 horse camps, and 106 miles of horse trails. Three horse camps are on the Brownstown Ranger District: Shirley Creek (16 miles of trails), Blackwell (60 miles of trails), and Hickory Ridge (20 miles of trails). Youngs Creek Horse Camp (10 miles of trails) is on the Tell City Ranger District.

The Hoosier National Forest is located in the rolling hills of southern Indiana.

Brownstown Ranger District

Hardin Ridge Recreation Area, located on the south side of the 10,750-acre Monroe Reservoir, is a national forest campground. Camping is allowed year-round.

For Information

Brownstown Ranger District
608 W. Commerce Street
Brownstown, IN 47220
(812) 358-2675

Recreation Area Information

Hardin Ridge Recreation Area is a 1,200-acre recreational complex located in southern Indiana's wooded hills on the south side of the 10,750-acre Monroe Reservoir. It is east of S.R. 446; accessible from the north via S.R. 46 east of Bloomington, and from the south via U.S. 50 east of Bedford. Hardin Ridge offers family camping, picnicking, boating, swimming, nature walks, and interpretive programs in a forested environment.

The recreation area has a total of 198 campsites, either for trailer/tent or tent-only/walk-in, at 6 campgrounds: Eads, Holland Ridge, Southern Point, Blue Gill, White Oak, and Pine. Each campground has piped water at central locations with flush toilets and showers. Electricity is available on one loop. Though some loops may be closed, camping is allowed year-round. Full service is available April 15 through October 15. During cold months, there are reduced services (no showers or flush toilets); and no fee is charged for camping. Reservations are accepted for Eads Campground only; phone 1-800-283-CAMP. The beach and Visitor Center are open Memorial Day weekend through Labor Day; the picnic area and boat ramp are open year-round. Pets are permitted but must be on a leash or confined; only seeing-eye dogs are welcome at the beach.

Facilities and Activities

198 campsites (6 campgrounds)
   34 tent only walk-in sites
   electric hook-ups (one loop)
centralized water
flush toilets/showers
dump station
60 picnic sites
2 picnic shelters (reservations)
2 playgrounds
nature center/exhibits
amphitheater/weekend programs
300-foot swimming beach
bathhouse with showers
camp store/concessionaire
fishing
boating/water skiing
3-lane boat launch
¾-mile interpretive trail
3½ miles of hiking trails

Celina Lake and Indian Lake are both strictly fishing lakes; no swimming or gasoline motors are allowed.

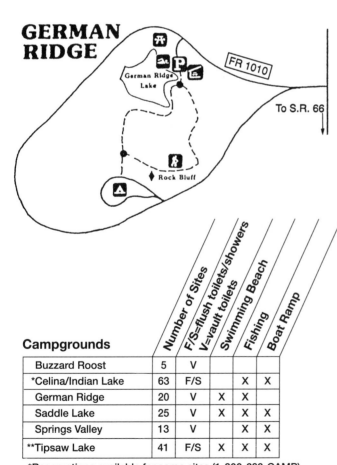

Campgrounds	Number of Sites	F/S=flush toilets/showers V=vault toilets	Swimming Beach	Fishing	Boat Ramp
Buzzard Roost	5	V			
*Celina/Indian Lake	63	F/S		X	X
German Ridge	20	V	X	X	
Saddle Lake	25	V	X	X	X
Springs Valley	13	V		X	X
**Tipsaw Lake	41	F/S	X	X	X

*Reservations available for some sites (1-800-283-CAMP)
**Group campground available (812/547-7051)

For Information

Tell City Ranger District
248 15th Street
Tell City, IN 47586
(812) 547-7051

Campground Locations

Buzzard Roost is a small primitive campground and picnic area at an overlook on the Ohio River; it is off of S.R. 66, north of Magnet on Forest Road 1960. There is no drinking water and there is no user fee; it is open year-round.

Celina Lake and **Indian Lake** are located about 3 miles from I-64 on S.R. 37 south; take exit 80. The 164-acre Celina Lake and the 152-acre Indian Lake are both strictly fishing lakes; no swimming or gasoline motors are allowed. Celina Lake has 2 campgrounds: South Slope is open April through November while North Face is opened as needed. The 12.2-mile Two-Lakes Loop Trail, that circles both lakes, is designated as part of the National Recreation Trail System.

German Ridge is located in the southern portion of the Hoosier National Forest, northwest of Rome and just north of S.R. 66. This was the first recreation area on the Forest; it has a 4-acre lake. The campground is open mid-May through November.

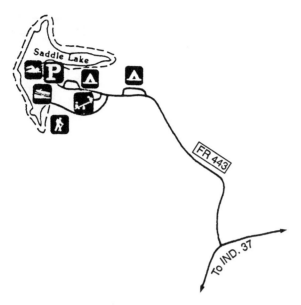

SADDLE LAKE

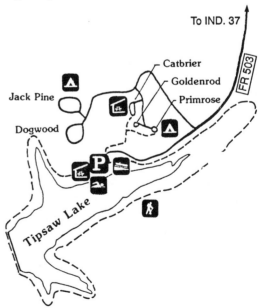

On the other hand, at nearby Tipsaw Lake, the swimming beach area is the center of attraction.

Saddle Lake is located northwest of Gatchel, off S.R. 37 and accessible via Forest Road 443; the lake has 41 surface-acres. The small primitive campground has 3 loops. The first loop is opened as needed and during deer season; loops 2 and 3 are open mid-May through mid-September.

Springs Valley, formerly designated as a Fish and Wildlife Area, was recently acquired by the Forest Service. It is located southeast of French Lick, accessible via county roads from S.R. 145. The 140-acre lake, surrounded by scenic hardwood forests, features primitive camping. There is no drinking water and there is no user fee; it is open year-round.

Tipsaw Lake is located about 7 miles from I-64 on S.R. 37 south; take exit 80. From S.R. 37, head west on Forest Road 503 to the campground and 131-acre lake. The campground has 5 loops. Two of the loops are family campgrounds, two are group campgrounds, and one is a campground with a shelter. Most facilities are open from mid-May through September.

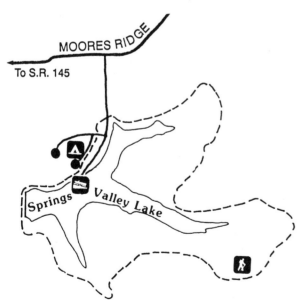

SPRINGS VALLEY
Not to scale

TIPSAW LAKE

Hovey Lake State Fish & Wildlife Area

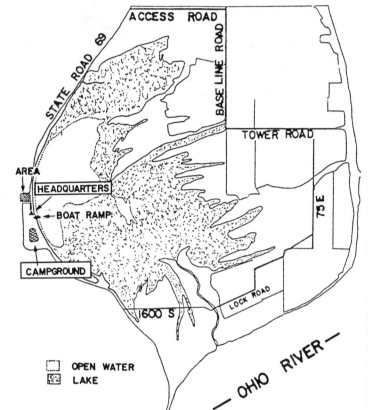

N

OPEN WATER

LAKE

The effort of these hardy ice fishermen has paid off with quite a catch!

For Information

Hovey Lake State Fish & Wildlife Area
R.R. #5
Mt. Vernon, IN 47620
(812) 838-2927

Location

Hovey Lake State Fish & Wildlife Area is located 9 miles south of S.R. 62 at Mt. Vernon via S.R. 69. The headquarters office is accessible off of S.R. 69; the campground is adjacent to headquarters. The Hovey Lake area is a 4,400-acre property that features a 1,400-acre natural lake, formed about 500 years ago when the Ohio River cut across a horseshoe bend. Because the property is in the Ohio River floodplain, much of the land is frequently underwater during late winter and spring. The slough areas to the east of the lake are much like a southern swamp.

Facilities & Activities

48 Class C campsites
  pit toilets
water, picnic tables & grills
picnicking
fishing/ice fishing
boating/canoeing
boat ramp
motor limit: 10 h.p.
boat/canoe rentals
hunting
limited berry, mushroom, nut gathering
hiking

Jackson-Washington State Forest

For Information

Jackson-Washington State Forest
R.R. 2
Brownstown, IN 47220
(812) 358-2160

State Road
County Road
Jackson Washington State Forest
Forest Office
Primitive Camping

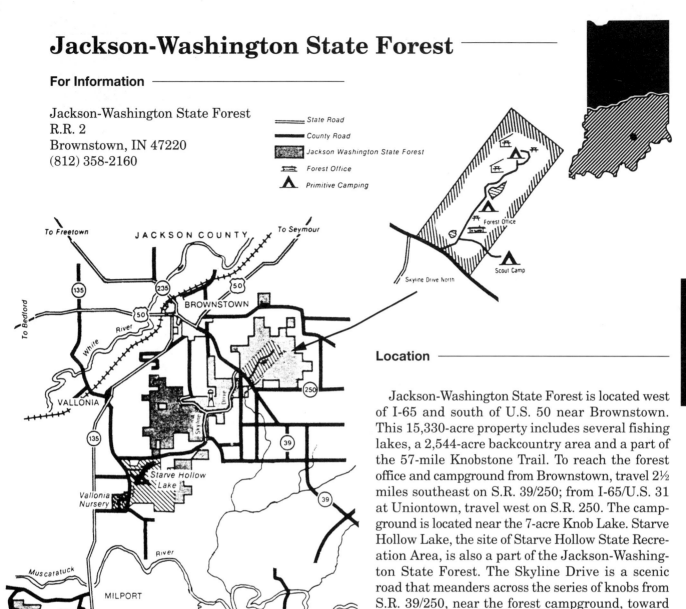

Location

Jackson-Washington State Forest is located west
of I-65 and south of U.S. 50 near Brownstown.
This 15,330-acre property includes several fishing
lakes, a 2,544-acre backcountry area and a part of
the 57-mile Knobstone Trail. To reach the forest
office and campground from Brownstown, travel 2½
miles southeast on S.R. 39/250; from I-65/U.S. 31
at Uniontown, travel west on S.R. 250. The campground is located near the 7-acre Knob Lake. Starve
Hollow Lake, the site of Starve Hollow State Recreation Area, is also a part of the Jackson-Washington State Forest. The Skyline Drive is a scenic
road that meanders across the series of knobs from
S.R. 39/250, near the forest campground, toward
Starve Hollow Lake; the road is very hilly and
treacherous, but the views are spectacular.

Facilities & Activities

70 Class C campsites
    pit toilets
youth tent area
backpack camping
picnicking, 3 picnic shelters
playground equipment
hunting, fishing, ice fishing
boating (electric motors only)
boat ramp
hiking trails (portion of Knobstone Trail)
bridle trails

INDIANA REGION 2

Jackson-Washington State Forest   57

Lieber State Recreation Area/
Cagles Mill Lake

Pontoon boats and houseboats appear to be more popular than speed boats at this marina.

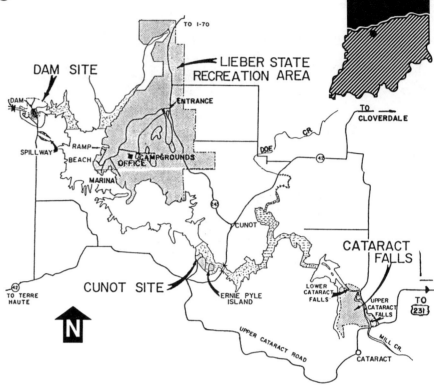

For Information

Lieber State Recreation Area
R.R. 1, Box 712C
Cloverdale, IN 46120
(317) 795-4576

Location

Cagles Mill Lake is roughly midway between Indianapolis and Terre Haute, just south of I-70. The lake is accessible from S.H. 243 or from southwest of Cloverdale on S.R. 42. This reservoir is known by 2 names: Cagles Mill Lake and Lieber State Recreation Area. The entrance to Lieber State Recreation Area is from S.R. 243; from I-70, take exit 37 and travel south to the park entrance. The park office is on the property.

Located on Mill Creek, Cagles Mill Lake is operated primarily for flood control in the Eel and White River watersheds. The lake comprises 8,075 acres; at the summer pool level of 636-foot elevation, 1,400 acres of water forms the lake and creates a pool length of 10 miles. The lake is maintained at or near permanent pool level except when flood waters are stored for flood control. The Mill

Creek Basin is located in relatively rugged terrain. Cataract Falls, the largest waterfalls in Indiana, is located at the eastern end of the lake and is accessible from S.R. 42 or U.S. 231.

Facilities & Activities

150 Class A campsites
   electrical outlet
   modern restrooms & showers
274 Class B campsites
   modern restrooms & showers
camp reservation system (3 major holidays only)
dumping station
camp store
naturalist services
visitor center
picnicking, picnic shelters
playground equipment
swimming beach
bathhouse/concessions
hunting, fishing, ice fishing
marina/motorboat rental
boating/waterskiing
3 boat ramps
2 miles of hiking trails

Lincoln State Park

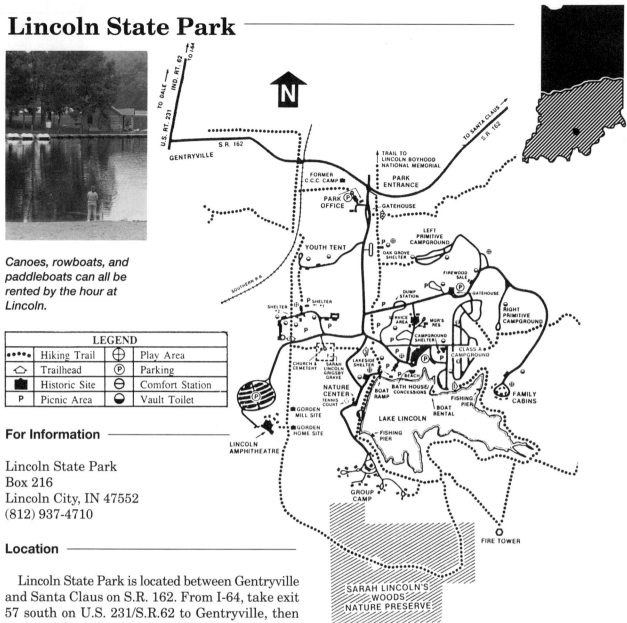

Canoes, rowboats, and paddleboats can all be rented by the hour at Lincoln.

LEGEND			
••••	Hiking Trail	⊕	Play Area
⌂	Trailhead	Ⓟ	Parking
■	Historic Site	⊖	Comfort Station
P	Picnic Area	⊖	Vault Toilet

For Information

Lincoln State Park
Box 216
Lincoln City, IN 47552
(812) 937-4710

Location

Lincoln State Park is located between Gentryville and Santa Claus on S.R. 162. From I-64, take exit 57 south on U.S. 231/S.R.62 to Gentryville, then east on S.R. 162 to the park. The 1,747-acre park includes a 58-acre lake. A 1,514-seat covered amphitheater was dedicated in 1987 to serve as the home of the "Young Abe Lincoln" musical outdoor drama. Across the road from the park is the Lincoln Boyhood National Memorial.

Facilities & Activities

150 Class A campsites
  electrical outlets
  modern restrooms & showers
120 Class C campsites
  pit toilets
campground reservation system
dumping station
camp store

group camp (155 capacity)
240-site youth tent area
3 rent-a-tents
10 family housekeeping cabins (each sleeps 6)
nature center, naturalist services
covered outdoor amphitheater
picnicking, 5 picnic shelters
playground equipment
tennis courts
swimming beach
bathhouse/concessions
fishing, fishing piers
boating (electric motors only)
canoe/rowboat/paddleboat rental
boat ramp
10 miles of hiking trails

Martin State Forest

For Information

Martin State Forest
P.O. Box 290
Shoals, IN 47581
(812) 247-3491

Martin State Forest features rugged hills, deep woods, and long hiking trails.

Location

Martin State Forest is located on U.S. 50 between Bedford and Washington. The entrance to the forest is 4 miles northeast of Shoals on U.S. 50. The campground is just north of U.S. 50; follow posted signs from the entrance. This 6,085-acre forest features rugged hills, deep woods, long hiking trails, and 3 small lakes, ranging from 2 to 4 acres. The forest offers a variety of educational opportunities to learn about sound forest management practices; they include an arboretum and the self-guided Woodland Education Trail.

Facilities & Activities

26 Class C campsites
   pit toilets
picnicking, picnic shelters
playground equipment
hunting, fishing, ice fishing
boating (electric motors only)
hiking trails

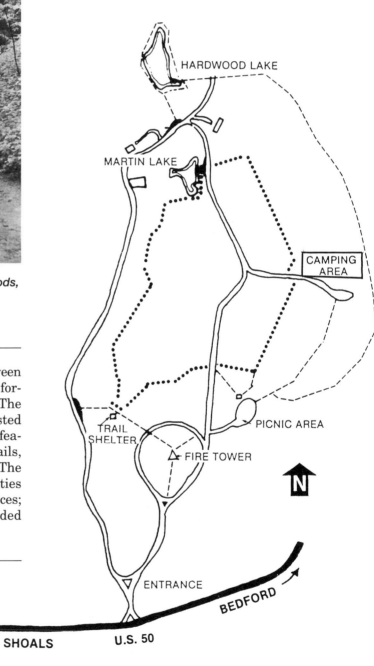

McCormick's Creek State Park

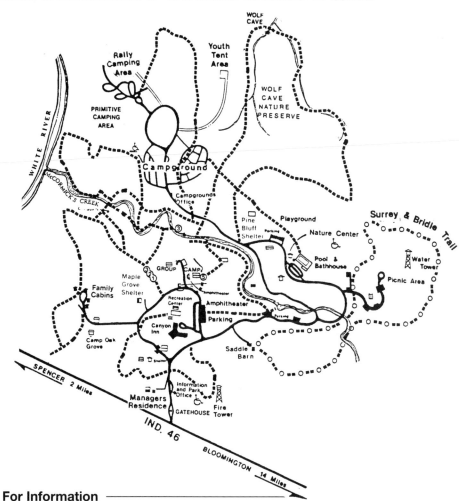

Just hiking in the rain!

For Information

McCormick's Creek State Park
Route 5, Box 82
Spencer, IN 47460
(812) 829-2235 (park)
(812) 829-4881 (inn)

Location

McCormick's Creek State Park is located 2 miles east of Spencer and 14 miles northwest of Bloomington on S.R. 46. McCormick's Creek State Park was dedicated as Indiana's first state park on July 4, 1916, as part of the state's centennial celebration. Magnificent canyons, high cliffs, unique limestone formations and scenic waterfalls are some of the highlights at the 1,833-acre park.

Facilities & Activities

189 Class A campsites
   electrical outlet
   modern restrooms & showers

135 Class C campsites
   pit toilet
campground reservation system
dumping station
4 group camps (20 each in 2) (100 each in 2)
60-site youth tent area
78-room Canyon Inn
   meeting & conference facilities
   dining room
   13 family housekeeping cabins (each sleeps 6)
nature center, naturalist services
amphitheater
picnicking, 9 picnic shelters
2 enclosed shelters (rentals 4/1–10/31)
recreation center, tennis courts
playground equipment
Olympic-size swimming pool
bathhouse, concession
8 hiking trails totaling 15 miles
bridle trail, saddle barn

Monroe Lake

Allen's Creek State Recreation Area

Paynetown State Recreation Area

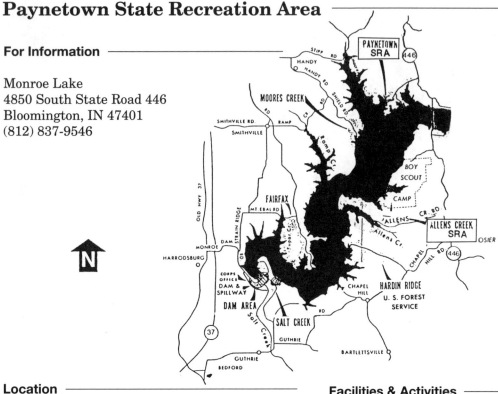

For Information

Monroe Lake
4850 South State Road 446
Bloomington, IN 47401
(812) 837-9546

Location

Monroe Lake is located about 10 miles south and east of Bloomington and is accessible from S.R. 46 (via S.R. 446) and numerous secondary roads that connect with S.R. 37. *Paynetown* and *Allen's Creek* are the 2 state-operated recreation areas that offer camping facilities. Paynetown has the most developed camping facilities; Allen's Creek has primitive sites only. Paynetown State Recreation Area is off of S.R. 446 just north of the causeway; this recreation area is also the site of the property's visitor center. Allen's Creek State Recreation Area is on a peninsula along the lake's south shore; it is accessible from Allens Creek Road off of S.R. 446.

Monroe Lake is on Salt Creek, a tributary of the East Fork of the White River; it is operated primarily for flood control in the Salt Creek and White River watersheds. Monroe Lake and environs comprise a total of 23,952 acres. At the summer pool level of 538-foot elevation, 10,750 acres of water form the lake and create a pool length of 37 miles. The entire area with its rolling topography, bluffs, scenic streams, and heavily wooded sections offers outstanding scenic vistas.

Facilities & Activities

	Allen's Creek SRA	Paynetown SRA
Class A campsites electrical outlets modern restrooms & showers		227
Class B campsites modern restrooms & showers		22
Class C campsites pit toilets		75
Class C campsites (walk-in or boat-in only) pit toilets	92	
camp reservation system (Labor Day & Memorial Day only)		X
dumping station		X
camp store		X
naturalist services		X
visitor center/wildlife exhibit		X
picnicking, picnic shelters		X
playground equipment		X
swimming beach		X
bath house/nature center		X
hunting, fishing	X	X
fish cleaning station		X
marina (fuel & rental docks)		X
boating/waterskiing	X	X
boat ramp	X	X
hiking		X

Morgan-Monroe State Forest

For Information

Morgan-Monroe State Forest
6220 Forest Road
Martinsville, IN 46151
(317) 342-4026

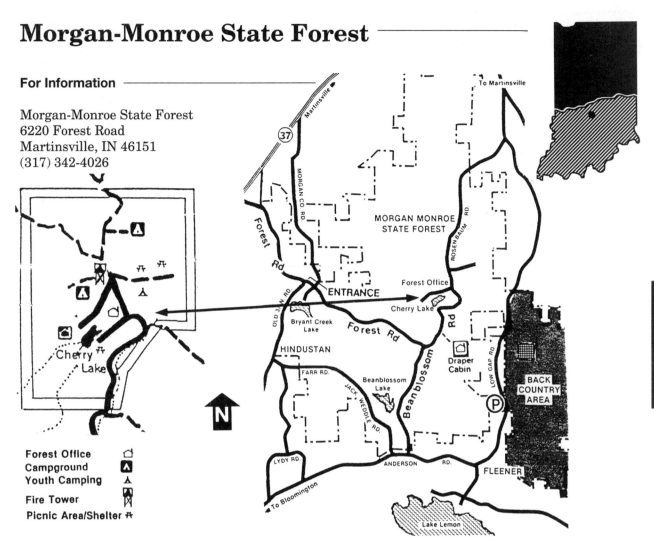

Legend:
Forest Office
Campground
Youth Camping
Fire Tower
Picnic Area/Shelter

Location

Morgan-Monroe State Forest is located between Martinsville and Bloomington on the east side of S.R. 37. The forest entrance from S.R. 37 is via Old S.R. 37 or Forest Road. This 23,443-acre forest includes 4 lakes ranging in size from 4 to 17 acres. Three primitive campgrounds are located just north of the forest office in the vicinity of Cherry Lake: Mason Ridge Campground, behind the fire tower, is open year-round for family camping; Oak Ridge Campground is open for overflow camping during busy weekends; and Scout Ridge Youth Campground is open year-round for youth groups. This forest is a popular place for hikers. There is a 2,700-acre backcountry area; trail maps are available.

Facilities & Activities

32 Class C campsites
  pit toilets
1 primitive rental cabin (April–mid November)
dumping station
6 youth tent areas
backcountry camping area
picnicking, 5 picnic shelters
playground equipment
hunting, fishing, ice fishing
boating (electric motors only)
boat ramps
4 marked hiking trails totaling over 20 miles

Trees, trees, beautiful trees—that's what state forests are all about!

Owen-Putnam State Forest

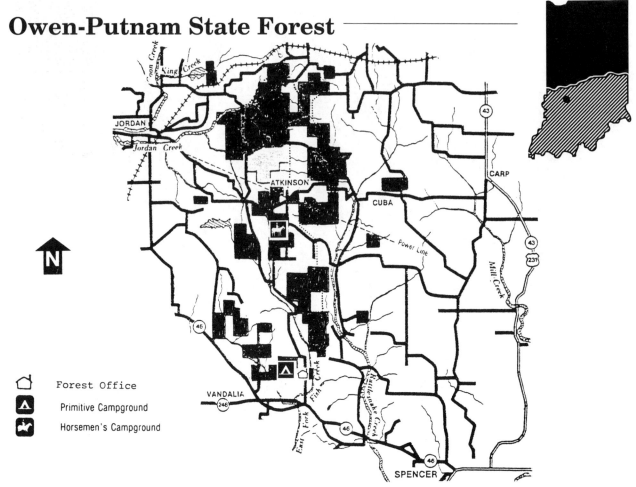

Forest Office

A Primitive Campground

🐎 Horsemen's Campground

For Information

Owen-Putnam State Forest
R.R. 4, Box 214
Spencer, IN 47460
(812) 829-2462

Owen-Putnam is one of seven state forests that has an equestrian campground.

Location

Owen-Putnam State Forest consists of scattered holdings totaling 6,236 acres, from south of I-70 to south of Vandalia on S.R. 46. The forest office is located just north of S.R. 46 between Spencer and Vandalia. There are 2 primitive campgrounds on the property: the family campground is adjacent to the forest office; the equestrian's campground is about 4 miles north via a county road, just south of the small town of Atkinson. There are numerous wildlife ponds at Owen-Putnam; many of them are fishable. This forest is a beautiful secluded place for hiking, especially in the spring and fall.

Facilities & Activities

14 Class C campsites
  pit toilets
20-site equestrian campground
picnicking
hunting, fishing, ice fishing
hiking on fire trails
horseback riding on fire trails

Patoka Lake/Newton-Stewart State Recreation Area

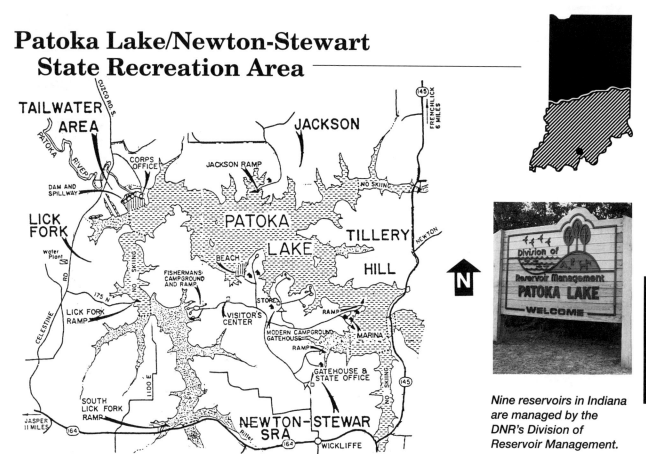

Nine reservoirs in Indiana are managed by the DNR's Division of Reservoir Management.

For Information

Patoka Lake
R.R. #1
Birdseye, IN 47513
(812) 685-2464

Location

Patoka Lake is east of Jasper and accessible from either S.R. 164 along the southern edge of the property, S.R. 145 running north and south along the eastern edge of the lake, or S.R. 56 on the northern edge of the lake. Entrance to Newton-Stewart State Recreation Area, the major recreation area, is off of S.R. 164. The visitor center, a unique solar-heated building, is located on the property. It offers nature displays, a bird observation room, and programs concerning solar energy.

The second largest reservoir in Indiana, Patoka Lake is operated for flood control and water supply and provides general recreation and fish and wildlife opportunities. The lake and environs comprise 25,583 acres; at the summer pool level of 536-foot elevation, 8,880 acres of water form the lake and create a pool length of 25 miles. The surrounding area of the lake consists of rolling topography, heavily wooded sections, deep draws, and scenic out-croppings. Numerous caves of significance lie to the east of Patoka Lake.

Facilities & Activities

450 Class A campsites (modern campground)
   electrical outlet
   modern restrooms & showers
   dumping station
   camp reservation system (3 major holidays only)
   camp store
96 Class C campsites (fisherman's campground)
   pit toilets
backcountry campsites
naturalist services
visitor center, wildlife exhibit
picnicking, picnic shelters
playground equipment
swimming beach
bathhouse/concessions
hunting, fishing, ice fishing
fish cleaning stations
marina/boat rental
boating/waterskiing
9 boat ramps
9¼ miles of hiking trails
bicycle trails
cross-country skiing

Pike State Forest

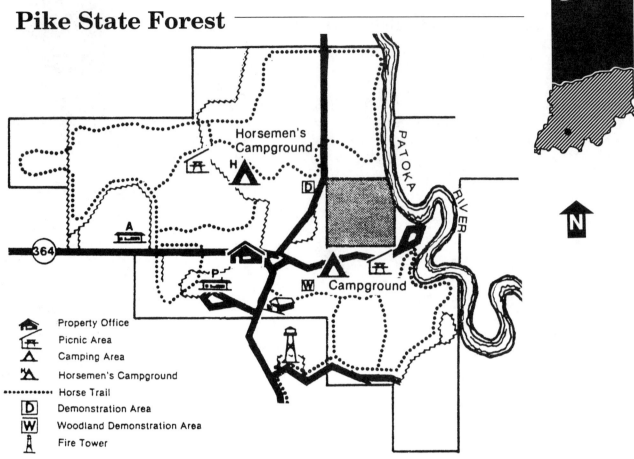

Legend

- Property Office
- Picnic Area
- Camping Area
- Horsemen's Campground
- Horse Trail
- D Demonstration Area
- W Woodland Demonstration Area
- Fire Tower

For Information

Pike State Forest
R.R. 1
Winslow, IN 47598
(812) 789-5251

Location

Pike State Forest is located north of I-64 and east of S.R. 61. From Winslow, travel south on S.R. 61 to S.R. 364, then east for 4 miles to the forest office. Both primitive camping areas are in the proximity of the forest office. The topography varies from the hilly uplands to the low bottomlands along the Patoka River. Because of this, a wide variety of plant and animal life can be observed at Pike. The river meanders through this 2,914-acre property, but boat access is difficult.

Facilities & Activities

11 Class C campsites
  pit toilets
25-site equestrian camp
picnicking, picnic shelters
hunting, fishing, ice fishing
15 miles of hiking trails
7 miles of bridle trails

Some photographers will try to walk on water to get a good shot!

Shakamak State Park

For Information

Shakamak State Park
Route 2, Box 120
Jasonville, IN 47438
(812) 665-2158

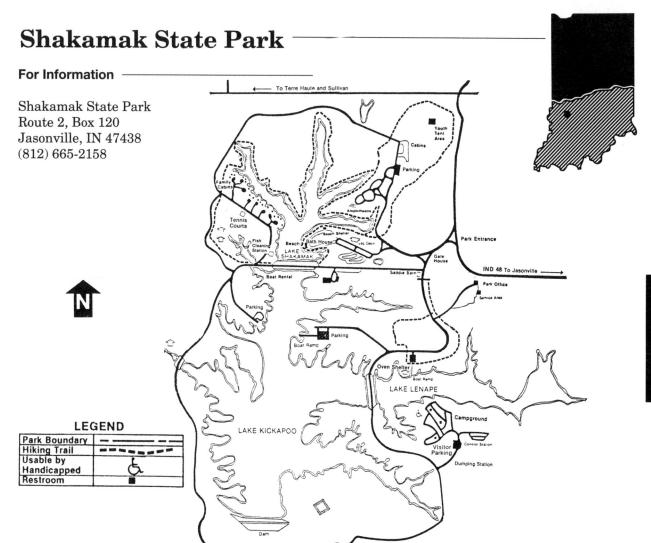

LEGEND

Park Boundary	— —
Hiking Trail	▬ ▬ ▬
Usable by Handicapped	♿
Restroom	■

Location

Shakamak State Park is located 2 miles west of Jasonville, on S.R. 48. Shakamak owes its name to the Kickapoo Indians. The Eel River, which is near the park, was called Shakamak by the Indians. Shakamak means "river of long fish," referring to the American eel, a delicacy of the Indians. The 1,766-acre park offers 3 lakes totaling over 400 acres of water for anglers to try their luck.

Facilities & Activities

122 Class A campsites
 electrical outlet
 modern restrooms & showers
74 Class C campsites
 pit toilet
campground reservation system
dumping station

group camp (270 capacity)
120-site youth tent area
28 family housekeeping cabins (each sleeps 4–6)
nature center, naturalist services
amphitheater
picnicking, 4 picnic shelters
log cabin shelter (year-round rental)
playground equipment
tennis courts
swimming beach, bathhouse
fishing, ice fishing
fish cleaning station
boating (electric motors only)
rowboat/paddleboat rental
boat ramp
bicycle rental
10½-mile bicycle loop
3 hiking trails totaling 5½ miles
bridle trails, saddle barn
horse rentals

Spring Mill State Park

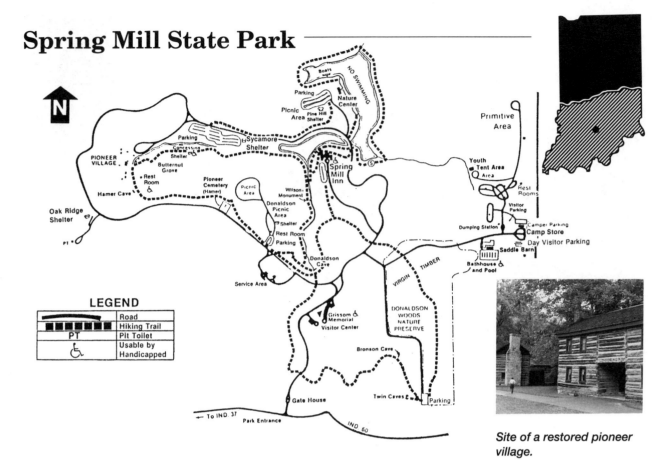

Site of a restored pioneer village.

For Information

Spring Mill State Park
Box 376
Mitchell, IN 47446
(812) 849-4129 (park)
(812) 849-4081 (inn)

Location

Spring Mill State Park is located south of Bedford, and 3 miles east of Mitchell on S.R. 60. The restored pioneer village allows you to travel through time to the early 1800s. The 1,319-acre park has 2 major cave systems and the waters from both drain into Spring Mill Lake, a 30-acre lake that is used for fishing and boating. There is also a memorial to "Gus" Grissom, a native of Mitchell, who was one of the 7 original astronauts and the second man to travel in space.

Facilities & Activities

188 Class A campsites
   electrical outlet
   modern restrooms & showers
36 Class C campsites
   pit toilet

campground reservation system
dumping station
camp store
120-site youth tent area
75-room Spring Mill Inn
   meeting & conference facilities
   indoor/outdoor swimming pool
   dining room
   Spring Mill Theatre
nature center, naturalist services
   boat rides in Twin Caves (April–October)
   walking tours into Bronson & Donaldson Caves
pioneer village
Grissom Memorial
picnicking, 5 picnic shelters
playground equipment
tennis courts
Olympic-size swimming pool, bathhouse
fishing, ice fishing
boating (electric motors only)
boat ramp
waterskiing
canoe/rowboat/paddleboat rental
5 hiking trails totaling 6½ miles
saddle barn
horse rental

Starve Hollow State Recreation Area

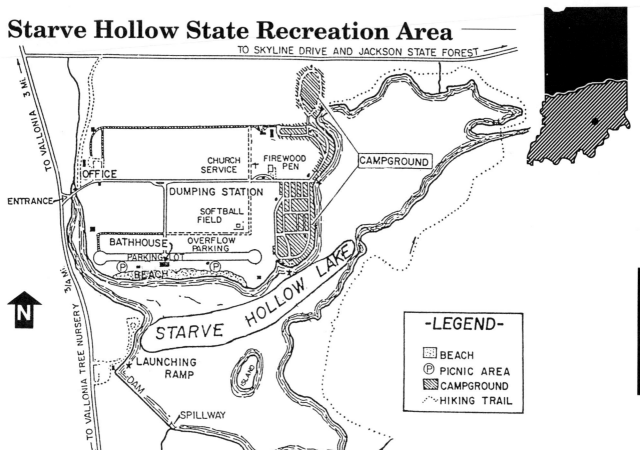

For Information

Starve Hollow State Recreation Area
R.R. 1
Vallonia, IN 47281
(812) 358-3464

Location

Starve Hollow State Recreation Area is part of the Jackson-Washington State Forest and is located 3 miles southeast of Vallonia on a marked county road that junctions at S.R. 135 in Vallonia. Vallonia is located 5 miles southwest of U.S. 50 near Brownstown. This 300-acre recreation area features a 145-acre lake, well-known for fishing, swimming, and its sandy beach.

Facilities & Activities

55 Class A campsites
  electrical outlet
  modern restrooms & showers
168 Class B campsites
  modern restrooms & showers
dumping station
nature center, naturalist services
picnicking, 2 picnic shelters
playground equipment
softball fields/volleyball
swimming beach, bathhouse
snack bar
hunting, fishing, ice fishing
boating (electric motors only)
3 boat ramps
canoe/rowboat rental
nature trail & hiking trail

Canada geese seem to love the lakes that allow electric motors only—maybe because they are quieter.

Sugar Ridge State Fish & Wildlife Area

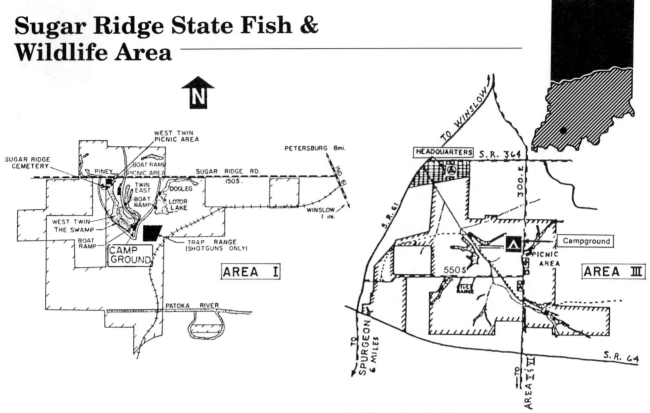

For Information

Sugar Ridge State Fish & Wildlife Area
R.R. #1, Box 314
Winslow, IN 47598
(812) 789-2724

Location

Sugar Ridge State Fish & Wildlife Area (formerly Patoka) is made up of 6 separate areas, totaling approximately 7,300 acres. About half of the land has been strip-mined; it features about 100 pits and lakes, along with rows of mounds of overburden from the mining operation. The land that has not been mined is mostly rough and rolling. The headquarters is located on Area III, which is south of Winslow, near the intersection of S.R. 61 and S.R. 364. One campground is on Area III, southeast of headquarters via area roads; another is on Area I, west of S.R. 61 via Sugar Ridge Road (County Road 150S). Maps to the 6 areas and other information are available at headquarters. Fishermen should ask for the *Fishing Guide* to the Sugar Ridge area; this free guide explains how to get to the 95 strip pits, their size, species of fish available, and boat ramp access.

Shoreline fishing, ideal for all ages, is available at some of the Sugar Ridge pits.

Facilities & Activities

13 Class C campsites (Area I)
   pit toilets
   NO water
   picnic tables & grills
13 Class C campsites (Area III)
   pit toilets
   water available, seasonal
   picnic tables & grills
picnicking
fishing, ice fishing
boating/canoeing
motor limit: electric only, 12-volt max.
boat ramps
hunting
shooting, archery range
berry, mushroom, nut gathering
hiking

Versailles State Park

For Information

Versailles State Park
Box 205
Versailles, IN 47042
(812) 689-6424

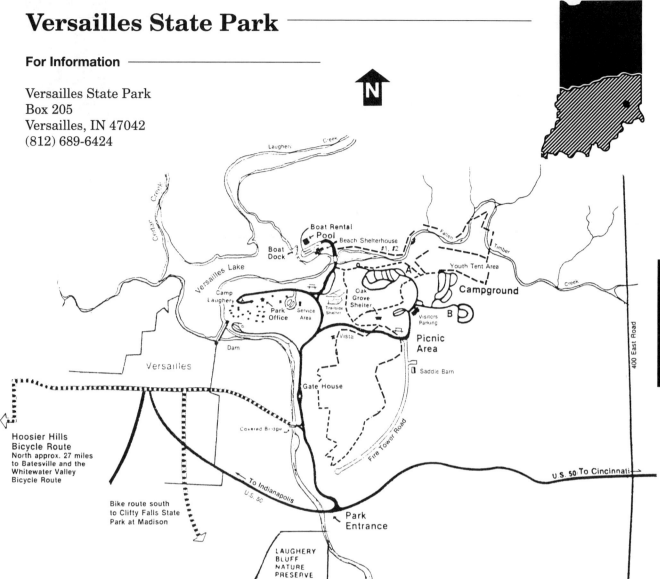

Location

Versailles State Park is located on U.S. 50, just east of the town of Versailles where U.S. 421 and U.S. 50 intersect. The 5,905-acre park features scenic hillsides with limestone outcroppings and winding stream valleys. Versailles Lake, a 230-acre lake, was created by impounding the waters of Laughery Creek, Cedar Creek, and Fallen Timber Creek behind an earthern dam.

Facilities & Activities

226 Class A campsites
  electrical outlet
  modern restrooms & showers
campground reservation system
dumping station
camp store, concession
group camp (120 capacity)
120-site youth tent area
naturalist services
picnicking, 4 picnic shelters
recreation building (year-round rental)
playground equipment
swimming pool complex, bathhouse
figure-eight water slide
fishing, ice fishing
boating (electric motors only)
boat ramp
canoe/rowboat/paddleboat rental
access to the 27-mile Hoosier Hills Bicycle Route
3 hiking trails totaling 6½ miles
bridle trails, saddle barn
horse rental

Whitewater Memorial State Park

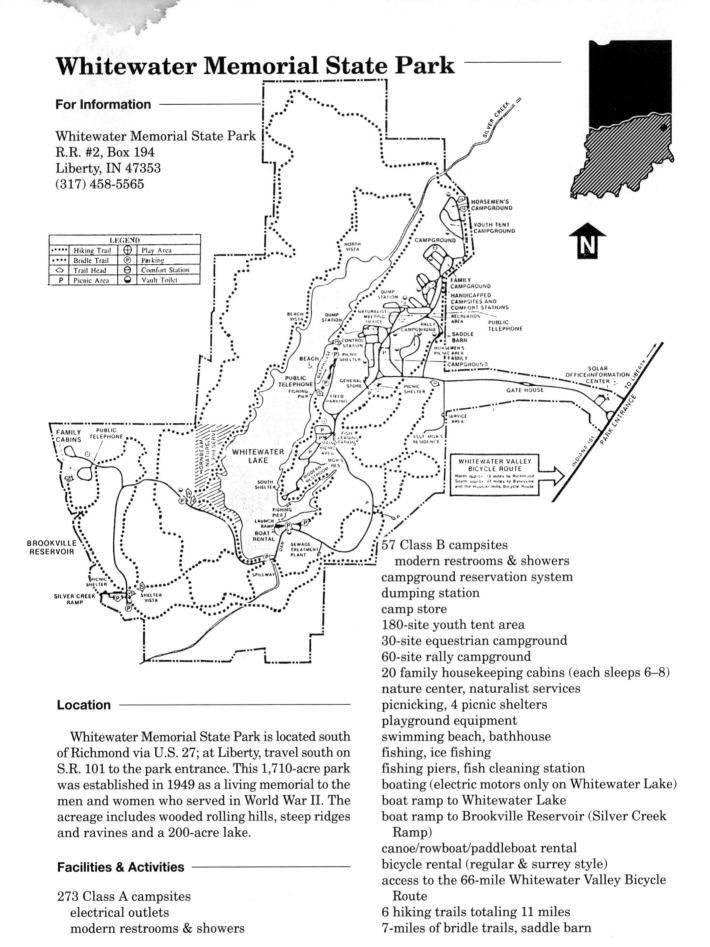

For Information

Whitewater Memorial State Park
R.R. #2, Box 194
Liberty, IN 47353
(317) 458-5565

LEGEND

••••	Hiking Trail	⊕	Play Area
••••	Bridle Trail	Ⓟ	Parking
⌂	Trail Head	⊖	Comfort Station
P	Picnic Area	⊝	Vault Toilet

N

Location

Whitewater Memorial State Park is located south of Richmond via U.S. 27; at Liberty, travel south on S.R. 101 to the park entrance. This 1,710-acre park was established in 1949 as a living memorial to the men and women who served in World War II. The acreage includes wooded rolling hills, steep ridges and ravines and a 200-acre lake.

Facilities & Activities

273 Class A campsites
    electrical outlets
    modern restrooms & showers

57 Class B campsites
    modern restrooms & showers
campground reservation system
dumping station
camp store
180-site youth tent area
30-site equestrian campground
60-site rally campground
20 family housekeeping cabins (each sleeps 6–8)
nature center, naturalist services
picnicking, 4 picnic shelters
playground equipment
swimming beach, bathhouse
fishing, ice fishing
fishing piers, fish cleaning station
boating (electric motors only on Whitewater Lake)
boat ramp to Whitewater Lake
boat ramp to Brookville Reservoir (Silver Creek
    Ramp)
canoe/rowboat/paddleboat rental
bicycle rental (regular & surrey style)
access to the 66-mile Whitewater Valley Bicycle
    Route
6 hiking trails totaling 11 miles
7-miles of bridle trails, saddle barn

Wyandotte Woods State Recreation Area

For Information

Wyandotte Woods State Recreation Area
7240 Old Forest Road
Corydon, IN 47112
(812) 738-8232

Pine Lake

Shelter House
Picnic Area
Fire Tower
Swimming Pool
Boat Ramp

Property Office
Parking
Public Telephone
Trailer Sites
Group Camping
Primitive Camping
Horsemen's Camp
Water Supply

The Pine Lake picnic area is located near the entrance.

Location

Wyandotte Woods State Recreation Area is located on the north highlands of the Ohio River within the Harrison-Crawford State Forest. The entrance to this 2,000-acre recreation area is on S.R. 462. From I-64 take the Corydon exit (#105) and follow S.R. 135 south to S.R. 62. Travel west on S.R. 62 for about 7 miles, then south on S.R. 462 to the forest office. Wyandotte Woods SRA provides one of the few modern recreation areas in a state forest. The campground, pool, and picnic areas are all located in lush forested areas.

Facilities & Activities

281 Class A campsites
   electrical outlets
   modern restrooms & showers

campground reservation system
dumping station
camp store
group camp (capacity 100)
120-site equestrian camp (Class C)
nature center, naturalist services
picnicking, 4 picnic shelters
playground equipment
Olympic-size swimming pool
snack bar
hunting, fishing, ice fishing
boating/canoeing
boat ramp (access to Ohio River)
canoe rental (available nearby)
hiking trails
bridle trails

Yellowwood State Forest

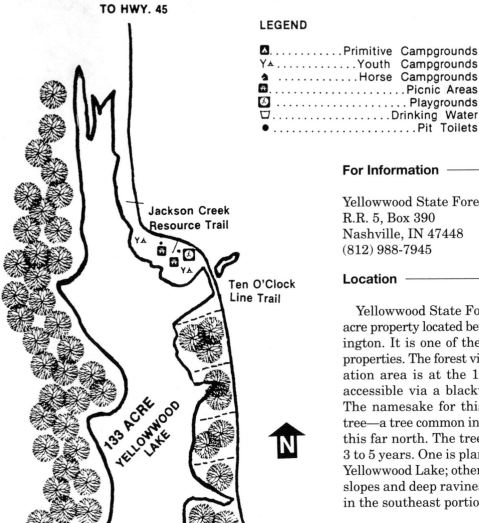

TO HWY. 45

LEGEND

🔺.............Primitive Campgrounds
Y🔺.............Youth Campgrounds
🔺.............Horse Campgrounds
🖼️.............Picnic Areas
🛝.............Playgrounds
🥤.............Drinking Water
●.............Pit Toilets

Jackson Creek Resource Trail

Ten O'Clock Line Trail

133 ACRE YELLOWWOOD LAKE

N

VISITOR CENTER

BOAT RENTAL

SHELTER HOUSE

DAM

SPILLWAY

BOAT RAMP

High King Hill Trail

TO HWY. 46

For Information

Yellowwood State Forest
R.R. 5, Box 390
Nashville, IN 47448
(812) 988-7945

Location

Yellowwood State Forest is a sprawling 22,508-acre property located between Nashville and Bloomington. It is one of the most popular state forest properties. The forest visitor center and main recreation area is at the 133-acre Yellowwood Lake, accessible via a blacktop road north of S.R. 46. The namesake for this forest is the yellowwood tree—a tree common in the midsouth but very rare this far north. The tree flowers abundantly every 3 to 5 years. One is planted at the visitor center at Yellowwood Lake; others are found on north-facing slopes and deep ravines near Crooked Creek Lake in the southeast portion of the forest.

Facilities & Activities

80 Class C campsites
   pit toilets
unlimited tents-only group campsite
6-site equestrian camp
visitor center
picnicking, picnic shelter
concession
playground equipment
hunting, fishing, ice fishing
boating (electric motors only)
boat ramp
rowboat rental
4 marked hiking trails totaling 19 miles
horseback riding on fire trails

Ohio Region 1

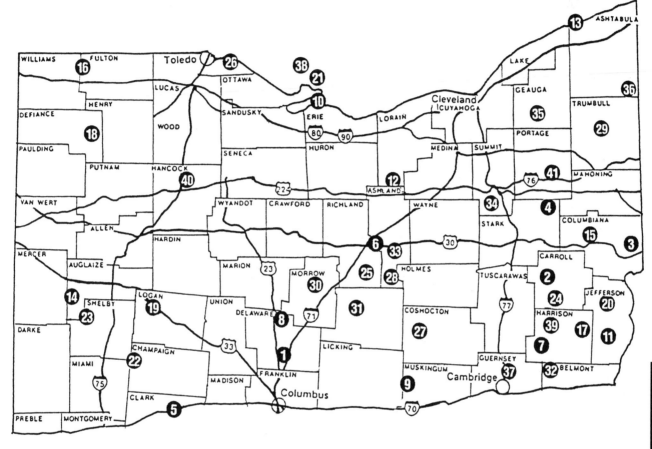

Alum Creek State Park

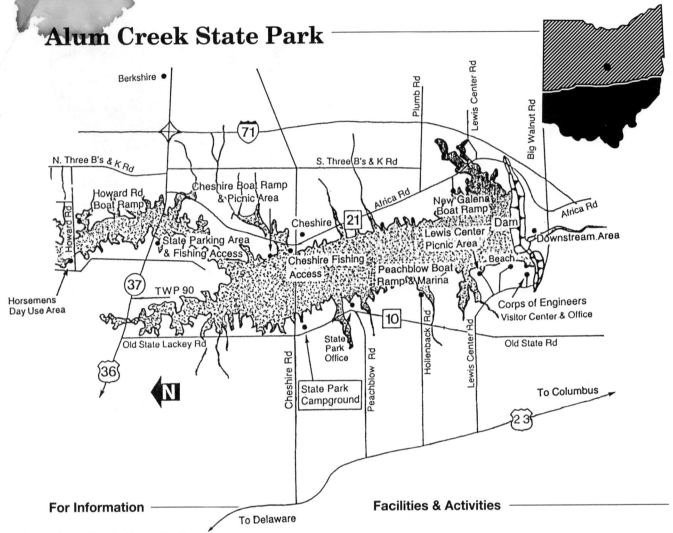

For Information

Alum Creek State Park
3615 S. Old State Road
Delaware, OH 43015
(615) 548-4631
(614) 548-4039 (camp office)

Location

Alum Creek State Park is located north of Columbus and southwest of Delaware. From the east, access is from I-71 at exit 131, which is U.S. 36/S.R. 37; from the west, access is from U.S. 23 between the I-270 loop north of Columbus and Delaware. The recreational facilities at this 5,213-acre park are at various locations around the lake. The park office and campground are both on the west side of the lake on C.R. 10; the campground is just north of Cheshire Road that crosses the lake. The popularity of this park is attributed to its 3,387-acre lake. Boats of unlimited horsepower, sailboats, canoes, and rowboats are permitted; the northern end of the lake is full of hidden coves and quiet fishing spots accessible only to the small boat.

Facilities & Activities

297 camping sites with electricity
5 rent-a-camp sites
showers/flush toilets
dump station
2 beaches at campground
boat dock/tie-ups at campground
boat launch at campground
pet camping area
picnicking
summer nature programs
3,000-foot swimming beach
beach concession
hunting, fishing, ice fishing
boating/water skiing
5 boat ramps
boat rental/seasonal dock rental
boat fuel/food service
snowmobiling
cross-country skiing
sledding, ice skating, ice boating
9½ miles of hiking trails
50 miles of bridle trails

Atwood Lake

For Information

Atwood Lake Park
Route 1, Box 345
Mineral City, OH 44656
(216) 343-6780
1-800-362-6406 (lodge)

Location

Atwood Lake was constructed on Indian Fork Creek for flood control; it has a surface area of 1,540 acres, a shoreline length of 28 miles, and 2,996 land acres. The lake is northeast of New Philadelphia and west of Carrollton. S.R. 212 from I-77, exit 93, crosses the dam; S.R. 542 and local county roads also provide access to the lake's recreational facilities. *Atwood Lake Lodge,* a resort and conference center, is located south of the lake on S.R. 542. Facilities include a 104-room lodge, 17 shoreline cabins, dining room, 18-hole golf course, lighted par-3 golf course, indoor and outdoor pools, lighted tennis courts, heliport, and airstrip. The *campground,* located at Atwood Lake Park, is on the northwest side of the lake; access is from S.R. 212 via. C.R. 93. Atwood Lake Park and the Lodge are open year-round. Pets are permitted in designated areas.

Facilities & Activities

569 lakeshore and wooded campsites
hookups (electric; some full)
flush toilets/hot showers
group camping
vacation cabins (sleeps 6)
camper cabins
picnic area/grills
group shelter
playground
miniature golf course
swimming beach, concession stand
water coaster
activity/nature center
amphitheater
hiking trails
hunting, fishing
boating/waterskiing (25 h.p. maximum)
2 marinas/supplies/lunch counter
boat ramps/docks/rentals
cruise boat rides

Beaver Creek State Park

For Information

Beaver Creek State Park
12798 Echo Dell Road
East Liverpool, OH 43920
(216) 385-3091

N

TO ROGERS

Pine Ridge Trail
Primitive Family Camp
Picnic Area
Williamsport Chapel
Mill Pond
Leslie Rd.
Oak Tree Lookout
Gastons Mill and Pioneer Village
Park Office
Dogwood Trail
Picnic Area
Vondergreen Trail
LITTLE
C.R. 428
Sprucevale Road
Echo Dell Rd.
Latrines
Primitive Horseman's Camp
Bell School Road
BEAVER
Gretchen's Lock Trail
Fisherman's Trail
CREEK
SR 7
Primitive Group Camp
Hambleton's Mill
Ware Road
Picnic Area
T-962 Birch Road
Sprucevale Lookout
Cannon's Mill Road

Little Beaver Creek was the first river to be included in the state wild and scenic rivers system.

Location

Beaver Creek State Park is located northeast of East Liverpool off of S.R. 7. The campground at this 3,038-acre park offers a primitive camping experience; it is north of beautiful Little Beaver Creek. The park office is south of the creek and near Gaston's Mill, a restored water-powered grist mill. Surrounding the mill is the reconstruction of a pioneer village with a schoolhouse, church, cabin and blacksmith's shop, all filled with antiques from Ohio's early settlement era. The beautiful river, the first to be included in the state wild and scenic rivers system, provides a challenge for canoeists. Canoes may be rented nearby.

Facilities & Activities

55 camping sites
dump station
1 group camp (500 capacity)
90 equestrian campsites
pet camping area
picnicking
hunting, fishing
canoeing
ice skating
16 miles of hiking trails
23 miles of bridle trails

Berlin Lake

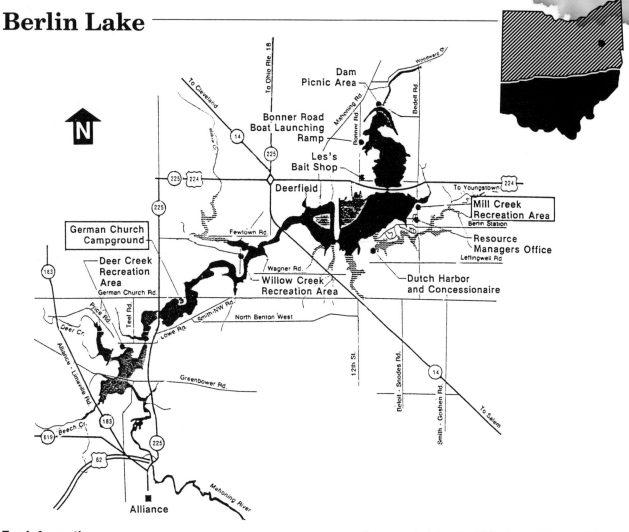

For Information

Berlin Lake
2030 Bonner Road
Deerfield, OH 44411
(216) 547-3781

Location

Berlin Lake, located on the Mahoning River, provides flood protection for the Mahoning River Valley as well as for the Beaver and upper Ohio Rivers. At summer pool, the lake is 18.6 miles long with a 3,590-acre surface area; the land area is 7,990 acres. U.S. 224 east from Akron crosses the lake just east of Deerfield. State routes 183, 225, and 14 cross the lake from north to south and give access to a number of recreational areas. Camping is permitted at 2 locations: Mill Creek Recreation Area and German Church Campground. Mill Creek is located on the east side of the lake, just south of U.S. 224; German Church Campground is west of S.R. 225 on German Church Road. The camp-

grounds, operated by the U.S. Army Corps of Engineers, are open from April 15 through October 15, exact dates subject to change.

Facilities & Activities

Mill Creek Recreation Area (fee)
   350 campsites
   electric hookups
   flush toilet/hot showers
   group camping area
   dump station
   swimming area
German Church Campground (free)
   primitive campsites
   drinking water
   swimming area
3 picnic areas
fishing
boating/waterskiing
7 boat ramps
marina, boat rentals

Buck Creek State Park

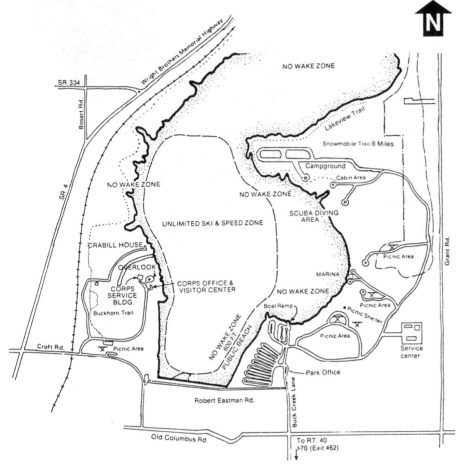

Sailing enthusiasts agree that the sailing at Buck Creek State Park is just great.

For Information

Buck Creek State Park
1901 Buck Creek Lane
Springfield, Oh 45502
(513) 322-5284

Location

Buck Creek State Park is located 4 miles east of Springfield off of S.R. 4; it is also accessible from U.S. 40 and from I-70, exit 62. The recreational facilities center around the 2,120-acre lake, offering endless water-related opportunities. The northernmost region of the 1,910-acre park is an excellent area to observe waterfowl and wildlife. The lake was built primarily as a reservoir for flood control. The park office is located on the east side of the lake; the Corps office and visitor center are located on the west side.

Facilities & Activities

101 camping sites
  89 sites with electricity
showers/flush toilets
dump station
26 family housekeeping cabins
pet camping area
picnicking, 2 picnic shelters
2,400-foot swimming beach
beach concession
scuba diving area
hunting, fishing, ice fishing
fishing pier
boating/water skiing
boat ramp/rental/seasonal dock rental
boat fuel/food service
snowmobiling
cross-country skiing, sledding
8½ miles of hiking trails

Charles Mill Lake

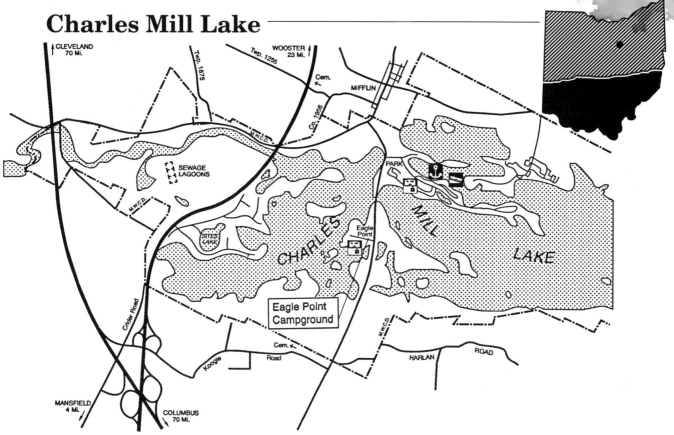

For Information

Charles Mill Lake Park
Route 4, Box 1271
Mansfield, OH 44903
(419) 368-6885

Location

Charles Mill Lake is east of Mansfield and south of U.S. 30. If approaching from I-71, take exit 176 and head east. The entrance to Charles Mill Lake Park is just off of S.R. 430 from Mansfield; also accessible by turning southeast on S.R. 603 from U.S. 30, then right on S.R. 430. The lake has a surface area of 1,350 acres and a land area of 1,997 acres. The full-service marina is located within the park, just northeast of the campground. Another campground, along with the camper cabins, are on S.R. 430 at *Eagle Point*. Every August, the Charles Mill Boat Parade attracts thousands. The campgrounds are open year-round. Pets are permitted in designated areas.

Facilities & Activities

510 campsites
electric hookups
flush toilets/hot showers
camper cabins
picnic area/grills
group shelter
playground
miniature golf course
swimming beach
hiking trails
amphitheater
hunting, fishing
boating (10 h.p. maximum)
marina/supplies/lunch counter
boat ramp/docks/rentals
40-passenger cruise boat rides

The Charles Mill Boat Parade attracts thousands of boaters every August.

Clendening Lake

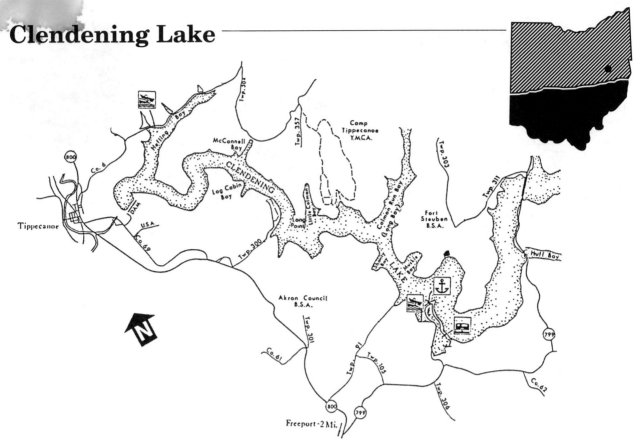

For Information

Clendening Lake
P.O. Box 116
Tippecanoe, OH 44699
(614) 658-3691

Location

The 4,750-acre Clendening Lake region has been designated a "natural wildlife area" and is to remain in an undeveloped "natural" state. Only a few access points are permitted. The dam to this 1,800-acre lake is just east of Tippecanoe near S.R. 800; the campground is located at the full-service marina on the lake's extreme south shore, just off of S.R. 799. Their season is April 1 through November 1. Pets are permitted in designated areas.

Facilities & Activities

70 campsites
electric hookups
motel
picnic area (near dam)
playground
hunting, fishing
boating (10 h.p. maximum)
marina/supplies/lunch counter
boat ramp/docks
boat rental

Truly a nature lover's paradise, Clendening Lake is designated as a "natural wildlife area."

Delaware State Park

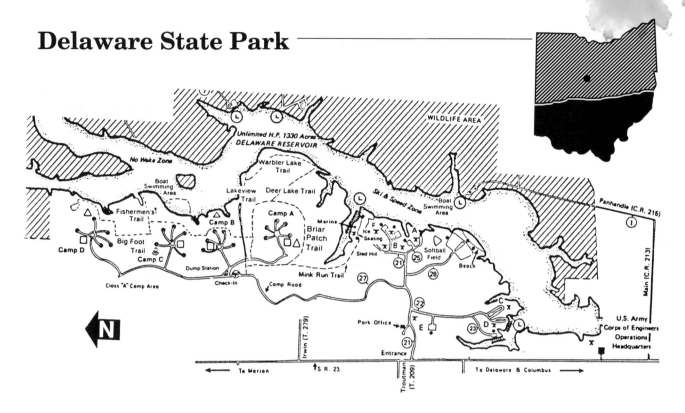

For Information

Delaware State Park
5202 U.S. 23 N.
Delaware, OH 43015
(614) 369-2761
(614) 363-4561 (camp office)

Location

Delaware State Park is located 8 miles north of Delaware off of U.S. 23. The park has 1,815 land acres within the reservoir complex, built as part of Ohio's flood control program. A portion of the scenic rolling land mainly along the east side of the reservoir has been retained in its natural state as a hunting and fishing reserve. The park and the 1,330-acre lake offer a diversity of recreational opportunities. In the summer, visitors enjoy the park's bluebird management trail. More than 90 boxes have been placed to attract this relatively rare bird and other cavity-nesting birds. Special interpretive programs about bluebirds are presented in the summer.

Facilities & Activities

214 camping sites
  164 sites with electricity
showers/flush toilets
dump station
laundry facilities
boat dock/tie-ups at campground
3 youth group camps (100 capacity; walk-in sites)
pet camping area
picnicking
summer nature programs
swimming beach, beach concession
hunting, fishing
boating/water skiing
boat ramps/rental/seasonal dock rental
boat fuel/food service
cross-country skiing
sledding, ice skating
5 miles of hiking trails

A portion of the Delaware Reservoir complex across from the state park has been retained in its natural state as a hunting and fishing reserve.

Dillon State Park

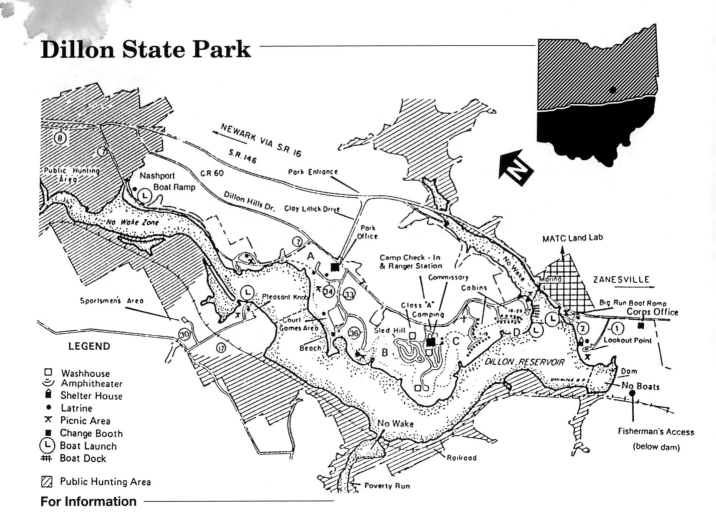

LEGEND

- ☐ Washhouse
- ☽ Amphitheater
- ◼ Shelter House
- ● Latrine
- ✕ Picnic Area
- ■ Change Booth
- Ⓛ Boat Launch
- ⊞ Boat Dock

- ▨ Public Hunting Area

For Information

Dillon State Park
P.O. Box 126
5265 Dillon Hills Drive
Nashport, OH 43830
(614) 453-4377
(614) 453-0442 (camp office)

Location

Dillon State Park is located 7 miles northwest of
Zanesville off of S.R. 146. The 1,660-acre reservoir, constructed for flood control, is a focal point
for many recreational activities. Thousands of land
acres have been set aside as public hunting areas
at this 6,030-acre park. A unique sports center is
on the west side of the lake; this area includes
trap and skeet fields, rifle and pistol ranges, and
an indoor small bore range. These facilities lend
themselves to weapons instruction and hunter
safety classes, shooting meets, and individual prac-
tice. Outdoor recreation is not limited to the summer season; there are beginner and intermediate
sledding hills, as well as a steeper hill and a warming area, all very close to the camping area on the
east side of the lake.

Facilities & Activities

195 camping sites
   183 sites with electricity
   12 walk-in campsites
showers/flush toilets
dump station
laundry facilities
camp commissary
boat dock/tie-ups at campground
29 family housekeeping cabins
pet camping area
picnicking, picnic shelter
summer nature programs
1,360-foot swimming beach
beach concession
hunting, fishing
sports center
boating/water skiing
4 boat ramps
boat rental/seasonal dock rental
boat fuel
sledding
10 miles of hiking trails

East Harbor State Park

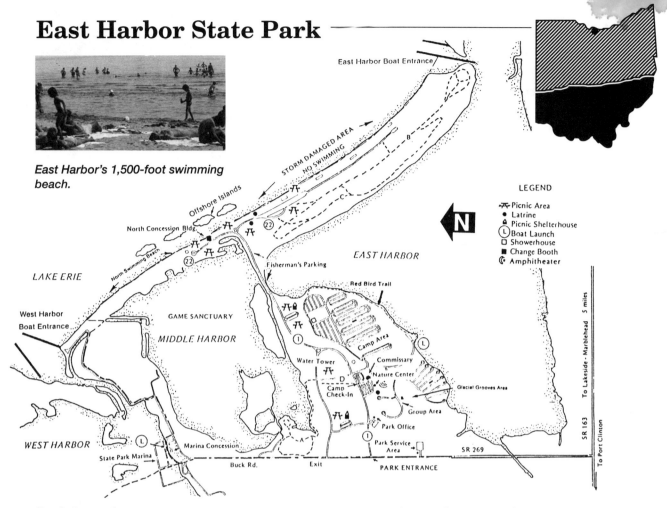

East Harbor's 1,500-foot swimming beach.

LEGEND
- 🛆 Picnic Area
- • Latrine
- 🛆 Picnic Shelterhouse
- Ⓛ Boat Launch
- ▢ Showerhouse
- ■ Change Booth
- ☾ Amphitheater

For Information

East Harbor State Park
1169 N. Buck Road
Lakeside-Marblehead, OH 43440
(419) 734-4424
(419) 734-5857 (camp office)

Location

East Harbor State Park is located adjacent to Lake Erie on S.R. 269; S.R. 269 is off of S.R. 163, which runs east-west between Marblehead and Port Clinton. The 1,152-acre park is situated on a peninsula shaped by the turbulent waters of Lake Erie's western basin. The campground is the largest in the Ohio State Park system. Boating access to West Harbor and Lake Erie is available from the launch at the park's marina; the launch ramp into East Harbor is for campers only. No boats with motors are permitted on Middle Harbor because it is designated as a game sanctuary. The park has a reputation as a great vacation spot, and not just in the warmer months of the year; during the winter, there are numerous cold-weather activities.

Facilities & Activities

570 camping sites
showers/flush toilets
dump station
laundry facilities
camp commissary
youth group camp (700 capacity)
picnicking, 2 picnic shelters
nature center
summer nature programs
1,500-foot swimming beach
beach concession
hunting, fishing, ice fishing
boating
boat ramp/rental/seasonal dock rental
boat fuel/food service
snowmobiling
cross-country skiing
sledding, ice skating
ice boating
7 miles of hiking trails

Fernwood State Forest

For Information

Fernwood State Forest
Route 1, Box 186
Bloomingdale, Ohio 43910
(614) 264-5671

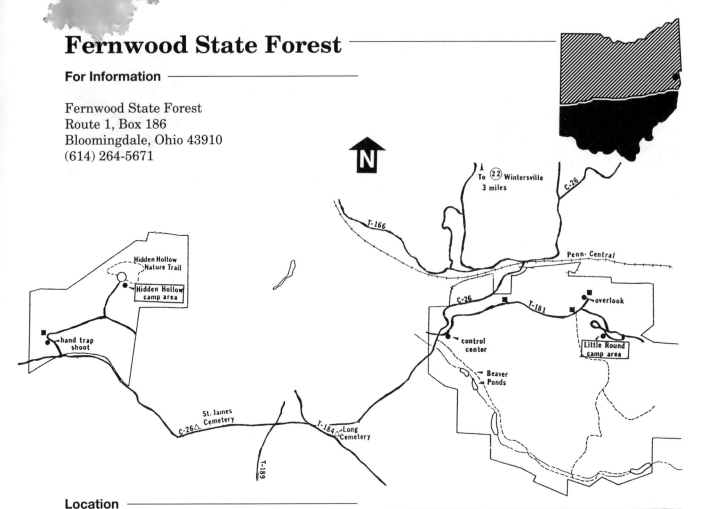

Location

Fernwood State Forest is located south of Wintersville and U.S. 22. The 2,107-acre forest is in 3 tracts. The 2 tracts that have campgrounds are off of C.R. 26; C.R. 26 is accessible via C.R. 25 southeast from Bloomingdale or from T-166 south from Reeds Mill to Fernwood. Hidden Hollow camp area is off of C.R. 26 just after turning left from C.R. 25 from Bloomingdale. To reach the Little Round camp area, continue east on C.R. 26 and turn right on T-181 before reaching Fernwood. Both campgrounds are fee areas.

Facilities & Activities

33 campsites
picnic tables
fire rings
drinking water
vault latrines
nature trail (Hidden Hollow)
3 miles of hiking trails (Little Round)
hand trap shooting area (Hidden Hollow)
hunting, fishing

Both campgrounds at Fernwood are fee areas.

Findley State Park

For Information

Findley State Park
25381 S.R. 58
Wellington, OH 44090
(216) 647-4490

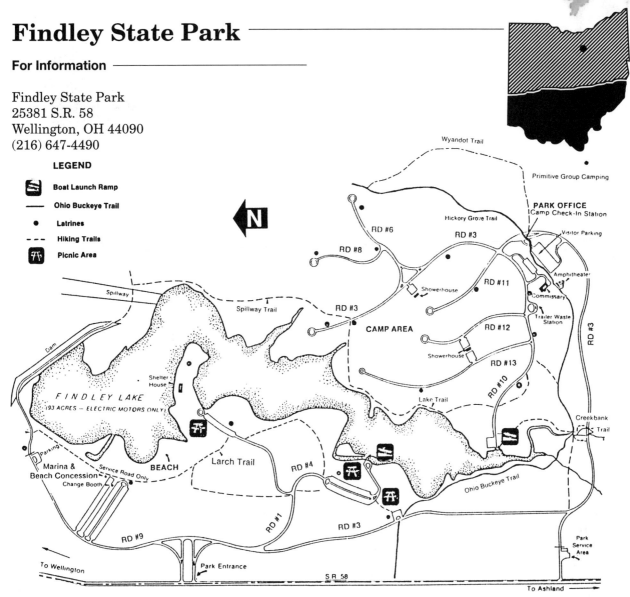

LEGEND

🚤 Boat Launch Ramp

—— Ohio Buckeye Trail

• Latrines

- - - Hiking Trails

🏕 Picnic Area

Location

Findley State Park is located 2 miles south of Wellington on S.R. 58. The park office and campground are located on the southeast portion of the 838-acre park, while the marina and beach are on the northwest. Canoes and rowboats can be rented at the marina for use on the 93-acre lake. Once a state forest, much of the park is heavily wooded with a wide variety of trees. The lowlands are excellent spots to view wildflowers, such as the marsh marigold and trillium, as well as migratory birds. One area of the park is set aside as a sanctuary for the Duke's Skipper Butterfly, an extremely rare insect.

Facilities & Activities

283 camping sites
showers/flush toilets
dump station
laundry facilities
camp commissary
boat launch at campground
3 rent-a-camp sites
youth group camp (40 capacity; walk-in sites)
pet camping area
picnicking, picnic shelter
summer nature programs
300-foot swimming beach
beach concession
hunting, fishing, ice fishing
boating (electric motors only)
2 boat ramps
boat rental/food service
cross-country skiing, ice skating
10 miles of hiking trails

Geneva State Park

For Information

Geneva State Park
Box 429, Pandanarum Road
Geneva, OH 44041
(216) 466-8400

LAKE ERIE

Swimming Beach
Boat Ramp
Beach House
Geneva-on-the-Lake Village
Route 534
Chestnut Grove Picnic Area
Snowmobile Staging Area
Lake Road West
Cabins
Route 534
Check-in
Cowles Creek
91-Site Full-Facility Campground
Wheeler Creek
Green Heron Nature Trail
Crabapple Picnic Area
Pandanarum Road
Maintenance Center
Rod & Gun Club Picnic Area
Park Office
Lake Road West

LEGEND

— · — Park Boundary
——— Public Road
* Restrooms
······ Trails

🏠 Picnic Shelterhouse
🎋 Picnic Area
☐ Change Booth

N

Location

Geneva State Park is located adjacent to Geneva-on-the-Lake on S.R. 534; S.R. 534 is accessible from U.S. 20 at Geneva and from I-90, exit 218. This 698-acre park is along the south shore of Lake Erie. Focal points in the park are the 2½ miles of Lake Erie beach, much of which is reverting to its natural state, and several areas of freshwater marsh and estuaries associated with the lake. Located in Ohio's snowbelt, the park offers an excellent base for snowmobiling on designated trails.

Facilities & Activities

91 camping sites with electricity
showers/flush toilets
dump station
laundry facilities
boat dock/tie-ups at campground
3 rent-a-camp sites
12 standard housekeeping cabins (5/1–9/30)
pet camping area
picnicking, 2 picnic shelters
swimming beach
hunting, fishing
boating
boat ramp
seasonal dock rental
boat fuel/food service
snowmobiling
cross-country skiing
3 miles of hiking trails

One focal point of Geneva State Park is the 2½ miles of Lake Erie beach.

Clifty Hills State Park is famous for its deeply cut gorges, sheer rock walls and plunging waterfalls.

White-tailed deer are frequent visitors to the campgrounds at Brown County State Park.

The fishing piers provided at Whitewater Memorial State Park give welcome access to the fish at the park's 200-acre lake.

On your next visit to Brown County State Park, consider picnicking at Ogle Lake; the setting is quite tranquil.

M. Little

Salamonie Lake has three recreation areas that offer camping facilities; Lost Bridge West State Recreation Area has the most developed campground.

Remember that campers who "sleep in" often miss the beauty of the early morning hour.

M. Little

J. Masterson

Fall is a delightful time of year to picnic at McCormick's Creek State Park . . . and then explore its canyons, cliffs, and waterfalls.

M. Little

Cagles Mill Lake, also known as Lieber State Recreation Area, is obviously a great place for houseboating.

90

Paddleboats, canoes, and rowboats are popular at Whitewater State Park because only electric trolling motors are allowed.

More than three-fourths of the campsites in Indiana's state parks are classified as modern sites with electrical outlets, showers, and restrooms.

Wooster Campground at Hardy Lake was designed primarily to serve fishermen and primitive campers; 19 class "C" campsites are available.

Like Potato Creek State Park, many of Indiana's parks have excellent swimming beaches.

M. Little

M. Little

Campers can beach their boats at Pokagon State Park, one of only two Indiana state parks that allow motorboating and waterskiing.

There is a noticeable lack of picnickers at McCormick's Creek State Park, but what a lovely day to leave footprints in the snow!

Kunkel Lake at Ouabache State Park is a great place to sharpen your fishing skills.

J. Masterson

M. Little

A good ol' friend and a good ol' boat guarantee a good ol' time fishin'.

Cedar Falls is part of the Hocking Hills State Park Complex that encompasses some of the most diverse and fascinating terrain in Ohio.

Seven state parks in Ohio provide equestrian camping areas, nine others have bridle trails for day-use only.

The popularity of Alum Creek State Park is attributed to its 3,387-acre lake. Plenty of fishing opportunities exist, even for youngsters like these.

Backpacking enthusiasts find the backpack trail at Burr Oak State Park both challenging and enjoyable. The 29-mile loop trail includes a portion of Ohio's 1,200-mile Buckeye Trail.

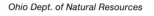

93

Ohio Dept. of Natural Resources

M. Little

Ash Cave, also part of the Hocking Hills State Park Complex, displays a 90-foot waterfall. A network of trails connect Ash Cove, Cedar Falls, and Old Man's Cave.

The picnic area at John Bryan State park looks especially inviting during the fall foliage season.

Ohio Dept. of Natural Resources

Lake Vesuvius Recreation Area, located on the Wayne National Forest, is adorned with beautiful trees as well as a beautiful lake.

Ohio Dept. of Natural Resources

Waterskiers abound at Pleasant Hill Lake; the campground and full-service marina are located on the north side of the lake.

94

At times it appears that the sailboaters and sailboarders at Kiser Lake State Park need a traffic director.

The two small lakes at Shawnee State Park are quite scenic; the campground and a picnic area are close to the beach at Roosevelt Lake, the smaller of the two.

During the annual Ohio Heritage Days, more than 100 historic farming and domestic skills are demonstrated at Malabar Farms State Park.

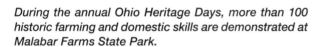

This limestone gorge, adjacent to John Bryan State Park, is cut by the Little Miami River; it is designated as the Clifton Gorge State Nature Preserve.

95

The forested hills of the Shawnee State Forest and Shawnee State Park, part of the Appalachian Plateau, have been dubbed "Ohio's Little Smokies."

Because of its beautiful surroundings, Scioto Trail State Park is said to be the ideal park for a "natural" getaway.

Is anyone in charge of this picnic in the park?

The type of water recreation possible on Ohio's streams and rivers is quite diverse; the canoeist can find rapid and wild water as well as calm and scenic water.

Grand Lake St. Mary's State Park

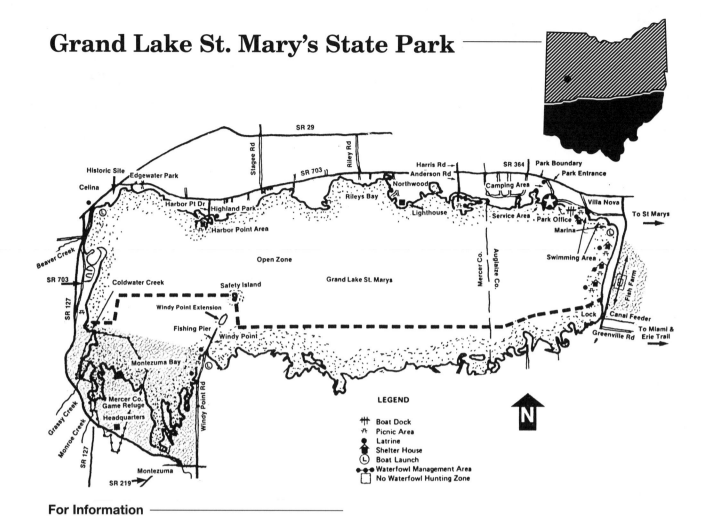

LEGEND

- ⚓ Boat Dock
- Picnic Area
- Latrine
- Shelter House
- Ⓛ Boat Launch
- Waterfowl Management Area
- No Waterfowl Hunting Zone

For Information

Grand Lake St. Mary's State Park
Box 308, Edgewater Drive
S.R. 703 W.
St. Mary's, OH 45885
(419) 394-3611
(419) 394-2774

Location

Grand Lake St. Mary's State Park is located 2 miles west of St. Mary's and adjacent to Celina on the southeast. The 13,500-acre lake, constructed from 1837 to 1841 as a feeder reservoir for the Miami-Erie Canal system, is a shallow lake. The lake can provide quite a spectacle in turbulent weather as its shallow depth can quickly produce large waves. Over 1,700 men worked on the digging of the lake; at its completion it was the largest manmade lake in the world. The adjacent 40-mile stretch of the canal provides excellent hiking and horseback riding on the towpath. The main recreational facilities of this 500-acre park are along the northeast shore, accessible from S.R. 703 and S.R. 364.

Facilities & Activities

206 camping sites
  50 sites with electricity
showers/flush toilets
dump station
laundry facilities
beach at campground
boat dock/tie-ups at campground
group camp (150 capacity)
picnicking, 3 picnic shelters
summer nature programs
4 swimming beaches
hunting, fishing, ice fishing
boating/water skiing
4 boat ramps
boat rental/seasonal dock rental
boat fuel/food service
snowmobiling
access to the 40-mile Miami & Erie Canal Trail (portion of Buckeye Trail)

Guilford Lake State Park

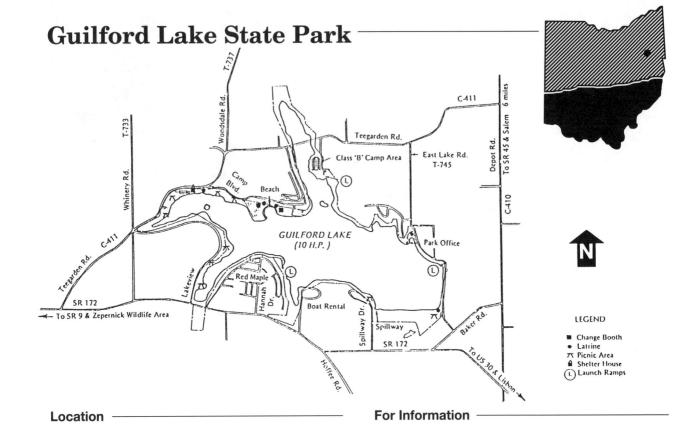

Location

Guilford Lake State Park is located 6 miles west of Lisbon off of S.R. 172 from U.S. 30. The 396-acre lake was originally constructed as a reservoir for the Sandy and Beaver Canal in 1834, but was later drained and used for farmland when the canal operation ended. The dam was rebuilt in 1932. The campground, on the north shore, is situated in an old pine plantation and provides shady areas at almost all sites; entrance is off C.R. 411 from S.R. 172. The popular swimming beach at this 92-acre park, located on the northwest side of the lake, is also off of C.R. 411.

Facilities & Activities

42 camping sites
dump station
boat dock/tie-ups at campground
picnicking, picnic shelter
600-foot swimming beach
fishing, ice fishing
boating (10-h.p. limit)
boat ramp
seasonal dock rental
ice skating

Guilford Lake provides a tranquil setting for those who take time to enjoy it.

For Information

Guilford Lake State Park
6835 East Lake Road
Lisbon, OH 44432
(216) 222-1712

Harrison Lake State Park

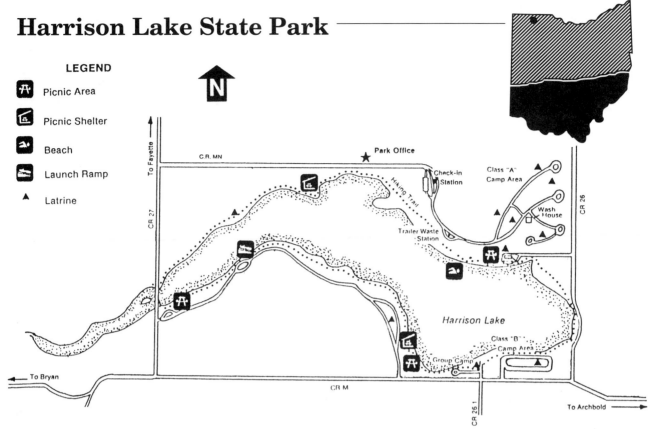

LEGEND

🏕 Picnic Area

🏠 Picnic Shelter

🏖 Beach

🚤 Launch Ramp

▲ Latrine

For Information

Harrison Lake State Park
Route 1
Fayette, OH 43521
(419) 237-2593

Location

Harrison Lake State Park is located 5 miles southwest of Fayette, accessible from the east on C.R. 26 and from the west on C.R. 27, both off of U.S. 20. The park office and Class "A" campground are on the north side of the lake, accessible from C.R. 27. The primitive campground and group camp are on the south side of the lake accessible from either C.R. 26 or C.R. 27; tall pine trees shade these sites. Rowboats, canoes, sailboats, and boats with electric motors are permitted on the 107-acre lake. Once the snow begins to fly, a variety of wintertime activities are also popular at this 142-acre park.

Facilities & Activities

178 camping sites
  126 sites with electricity
showers/flush toilets
dump station
laundry facilities
3 rent-a-camp sites
youth group camp (90 capacity)
pet camping area
picnicking, 2 picnic shelters
swimming beach
fishing, ice fishing
boating (electric motors only)
boat ramp
cross-country skiing
sledding, ice skating
3 miles of hiking trails

Ducks enjoy the lake's shallow western end.

Harrison State Forest

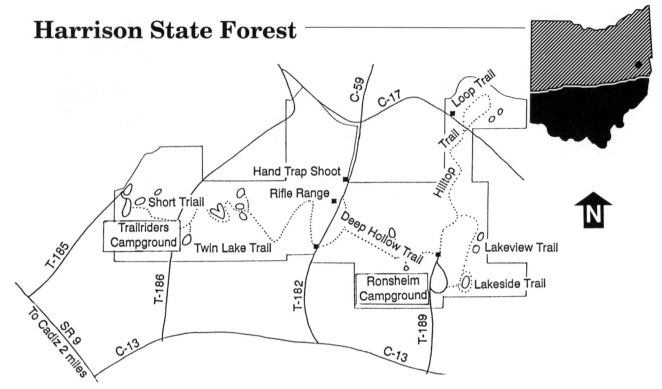

For Information

Harrison State Forest
c/o Fernwood State Forest
Route 1, Box 186
Bloomingdale, Ohio 43910
(614) 264-5671

Location

Harrison State Forest is located about 3 miles north of Cadiz, east of S.R. 9. The primary area lies north of C.R. 13, while 2 smaller tracts are located south of C.R. 13. The forest has 1,345 acres of land and some 15 small ponds; one is a 2-acre pond. There are 2 primitive campgrounds: Ronsheim, a family campground, and Trailriders, which accommodates horsemen or family campers; both are fee areas. Trailriders Campground is off of S.R. 9; when traveling north from Cadiz, go past C.R. 13 and turn right at the next road, T-185 (Camp Road). To reach Ronsheim Campground, turn right on C.R. 13, and turn left at T-189; this road is just past Briar Road (T-182) that goes to the rifle range.

A total of almost 250 miles of marked bridle trails are located in 12 state forests in Ohio.

Facilities & Activities

15 campsites at Ronsheim
22 campsites at Trailriders
picnic tables
fire rings
drinking water

vault latrines
4 miles of bridle trails
4 miles of hiking trails
rifle range
hand trap shooting area
fishing, hunting

Independence Dam State Park

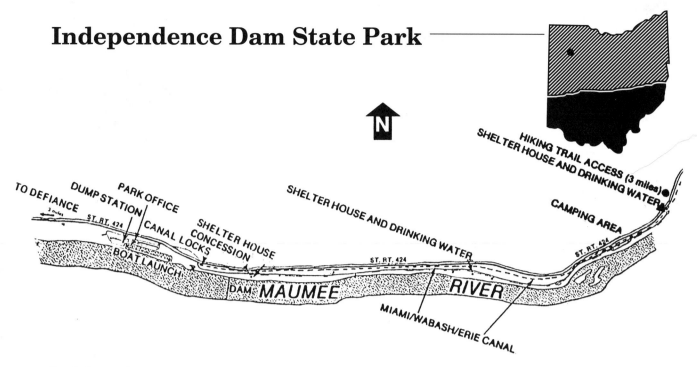

For Information

Independence Dam State Park
Rt. #4, 27722 S.R. 424
Defiance, OH 43512
(419) 784-3263

In the winter, cross-country skiing can be enjoyed throughout the park.

Location

Independence Dam State Park is located 3 miles east of Defiance along S.R. 424. The 604-acre park lies between 7 unbroken miles of the historic Miami and Erie Canal and the Maumee River. The main entrance road to the park crosses over the ruins of Lock Number Thirteen. The park office and a 4-lane launch ramp are located on the north bank of the river about 300 yards west of the dam; waterskiers enjoy 4 miles of water on the Maumee River. The 3-mile main access road, within the park, leads to a small, nicely shaded primitive campground along the scenic river. A hiking trail meanders between the old canal and the river for a distance of 3 miles. In the winter, cross-country skiing can be enjoyed throughout the park; ice skating is available on the canal, weather permitting.

Facilities & Activities

40 camping sites
dump station
pet camping area
picnicking, 2 picnic shelters
fishing
boating/water skiing
4 boat ramps
cross-country skiing
sledding, ice skating
3 miles of hiking trails
portion of the Buckeye Trail

Indian Lake State Park

For Information

Indian Lake State Park
7490 Edgewater Ave.
Huntsville, OH 43324
(513) 843-2098
(513) 843-3553 (camp office)

Location

Indian Lake State Park is located 12 miles north-west of Bellefontaine off of U.S. 33. Lewistown Reservoir was built in 1851 as a feeder lake for the Miami and Erie Canal; in 1898, it was dedicated as a state park by the name of Indian Lake. Indian Lake became a popular resort area at the turn of the century; today's popularity stems from the many recreational activities the 648-acre park has to offer. The 5,800-acre lake is the only inland lake in Ohio with lighted buoys for night navigation; 20 boat-camping spaces are also available. The park office is on the southeast side of the lake off of S.R. 366; the campground, that offers primarily sunny sites, is on the north side of the lake off of S.R. 235. Winter activities are popular; the areas known as the South and West Banks, as well as the frozen lake surface, may be used for snowmobiling.

Facilities & Activities

443 camping sites
  370 sites with electricity
showers/flush toilets
dump station
laundry facilities
camp commissary
beach at campground
boat dock/tie-ups at campground
boat launch at campground
2 rent-a-camp sites
group camp (360 capacity)
pet camping area
picnicking, 4 picnic shelters
summer nature programs
2 swimming beaches
hunting, fishing, ice fishing
boating/water skiing
4 boat ramps
seasonal dock rental
snowmobiling, ice boating
cross-country skiing, ice skating
2 miles of hiking trails

Jefferson Lake State Park

Camp Check
In Station

Service Center
Park Office

Parking

C-54

Nature
Center

Parking

Shelter
House

Picnic Areas

Bath House

Beach

Class "B" Camp
Area

Parking

Ball Fields

T-219

Hiking Trails

T-219

C-54

N

For Information

Jefferson Lake State Park
R.D. 1, Box 140
Richmond, OH 43944
(614) 765-4459

Location

Jefferson Lake State Park is located northwest
of Steubenville and 2½ miles northwest of Richmond, off of S.R. 43. The park office and campground are at the north end of the 906-acre park off
C.R. 54. Nestled in oak and hickory woodlands,
the tree-sheltered campsites offer privacy and
peaceful scenery. Hiking the miles of scenic, rugged
trails that meander through the park is a pleasure
to be enjoyed during any season. The 27-acre lake
is regularly stocked; access to the lake and the
public beach is off of the main access road, C.R. 54.

Facilities & Activities

100 camping sites
dump station
2 rent-a-camp sites
pet camping area

picnicking, picnic shelter
swimming beach
hunting, fishing, ice fishing
boating (electric motors only)
boat ramp
cross-country skiing
sledding, ice skating
10 miles of hiking trails

**OHIO
REGION 1**

The 27-acre lake is regularly stocked.

Kelleys Island State Park

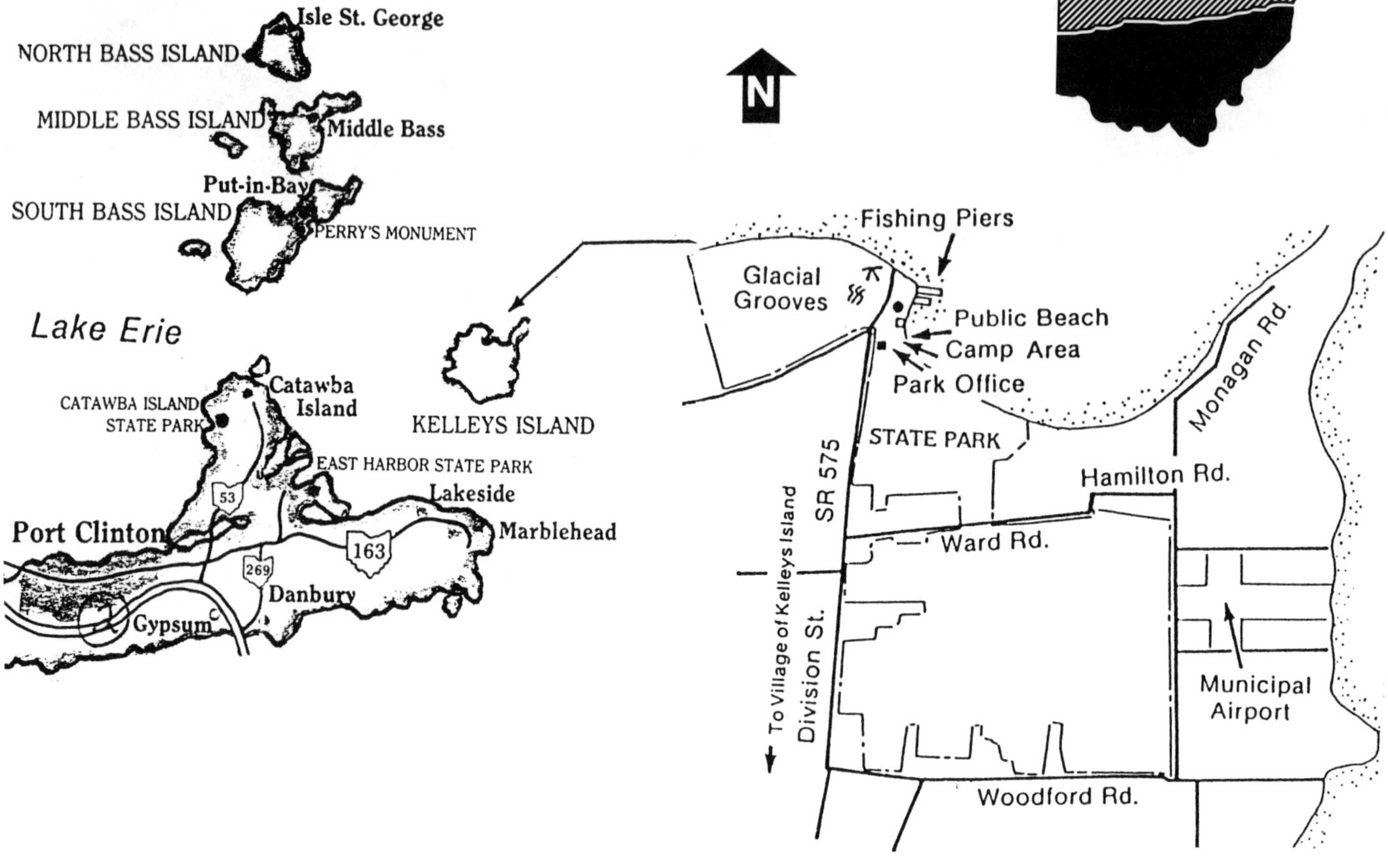

For Information

Kelleys Island State Park
4049 E. Moores Dock Road
Port Clinton, OH 43452
(419) 797-4530

Location

Kelleys Island is the largest American island in Lake Erie; it can be reached by ferry from Marblehead or from Sandusky. The 661-acre state park is located on the island's north side, at the end of Division Street (S.R. 575). The campground provides magnificent views of Lake Erie. The famous glacial grooves are located on the north shore near the state park; when the last glacier retreated just over 10,000 years ago, it carved 6-foot grooves into the bedrock. On the south shore there is a large flat-topped slab of limestone that has pictographs created by Erie Indians in about A.D. 1600; it is called Inscription Rock. There are hourly tram tours of the island plus regular bus service; also available for rental are golf carts, mopeds and bicycles.

Facilities & Activities

129 camping sites
showers/flush toilets
dump station
2 youth group camps (50 capacity)
pet camping area
picnicking, picnic shelter
summer nature programs
100-foot swimming beach
bicycling
hunting, fishing, ice fishing
fishing pier
boating on Lake Erie
boat ramp
snowmobiling
cross-country skiing, ice skating
5 miles of hiking trails

Kiser Lake State Park

For Information

Kiser Lake State Park
Box 55
Rosewood, OH 43070-0055
(513) 362-3822
(513) 362-3565 (camp office)

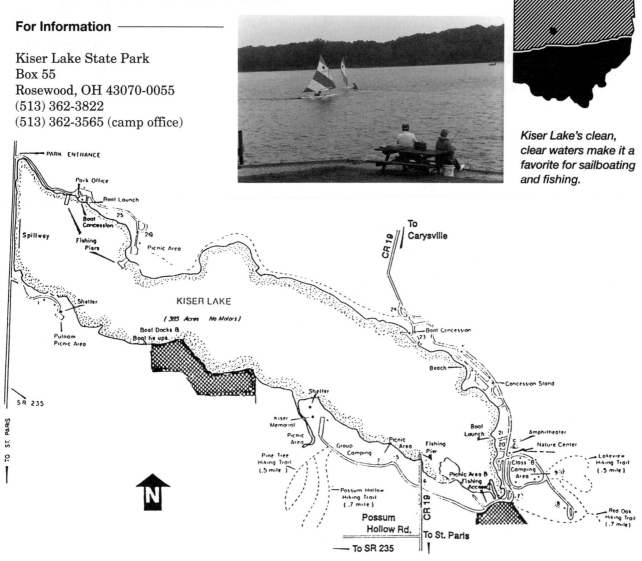

Kiser Lake's clean, clear waters make it a favorite for sailboating and fishing.

Location

Kiser Lake State Park is located 6 miles north of St. Paris on S.R. 235. The park office is at the north end of the dam and spillway. The campground, swimming beach, and other recreational facilities are at the southeast end of the lake, accessible from S.R. 235 via Possum Hollow Road, or from St. Paris via Kiser Lake Road (C.R. 19). The 396-acre lake, known for its clean, clear waters, makes it a favorite for sailboating and fishing. Five hiking trails, located within the 474-acre park, provide miles of walking pleasure; these trails lead the hiker through mature mixed hardwood woodlands.

Facilities & Activities

140 camping sites
dump station
2 rent-a-camp sites
group camp (300 capacity)
picnicking, picnic shelters
300-foot swimming beach
beach concession
hunting, fishing, ice fishing
fishing piers
boating/sailing (no motors permitted)
boat ramps/rental
sledding, ice skating
4½ miles of hiking trails

Lake Loramie State Park

For Information

Lake Loramie State Park
11221 S.R. 362
Minster, OH 45865-9311
(513) 295-2011
(513) 295-3900 (camp office)

Location

Lake Loramie State Park is located 1 mile south of Minster off of S.R. 66. The park office and the campground are off of S.R. 362, accessible from S.R. 66 via Canal Road or Ft. Loramie-Swanders Road. The campground at this 400-acre park has a unique island location in an open, sunny area. The 1,655-acre lake is one of five feeder lakes constructed as part of the vast Ohio canal system. High-speed boating is allowed in a special zone at the lake's west end; waterskiing is not permitted because of the limited lake area. Hikers can cross a foot bridge to Blackberry Island where a 1-mile trail passes through an oak woods offering a glimpse of a variety of wildlife. Lotus, a large water lily, thrives in the lake's undisturbed coves.

Facilities & Activities

184 camping sites
dump station
boat dock/tie-ups at campground
3 rent-a-camp sites
3 youth group camps (105 capacity; tents only)
picnicking, picnic shelters
summer nature programs
swimming beach
hunting, fishing, ice fishing
boating
boat ramps/seasonal dock rental
snowmobiling
cross-country skiing, ice skating
10 miles of hiking trails (access to the Miami & Erie Canal Trail and the Buckeye Trail)

Leesville Lake

For Information

Leesville Lake
5037 Deer Road, SW
Bowerston, OH 44695
(216) 627-4270 (Petersburg marina)
(614) 269-5371 (Leesville marina)

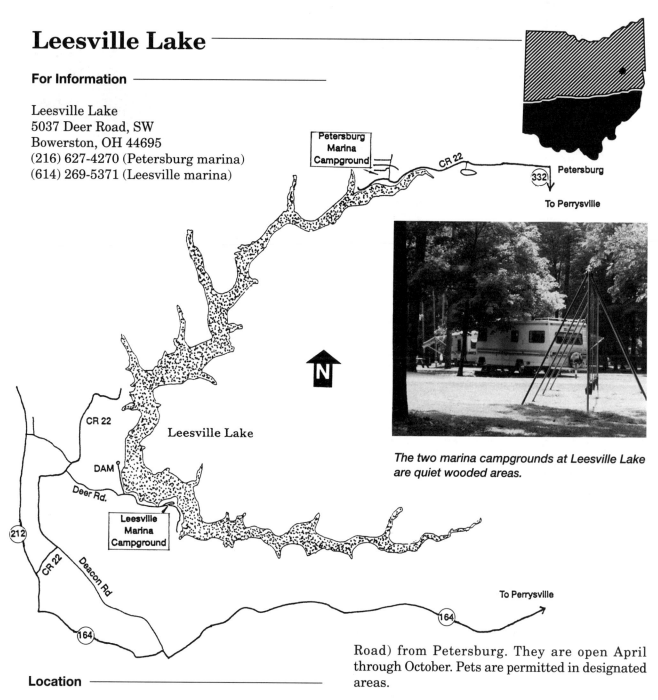

The two marina campgrounds at Leesville Lake are quiet wooded areas.

Location

Leesville Reservoir was constructed on McGuire Fork Creek for flood control; it has a surface area of 1,000 acres, a land area of 2,627 acres, and a shoreline length of 28 miles. The lake, located east of New Philadelphia via S.R. 39 and southwest of Carrollton via S.R. 332 has 2 marinas. These 2 marinas, Leesville (South Fork) and Petersburg (North Fork), are full service marinas; they also offer campsites in quiet wooded areas. To reach the Leesville Marina, travel north on S.R. 212 from Leesville, turn right on C.R. 22, then right on Deer Road; the marina is past the dam. To reach the Petersburg Marina, travel west on C.R. 22 (Azalea Road) from Petersburg. They are open April through October. Pets are permitted in designated areas.

Facilities & Activities

200 campsites
electric hookups
restrooms
camper cabins
marina fishing cabins
playground
hunting, fishing
boating (10 h.p. maximum)
2 marinas/supplies/lunch counter
boat ramps/docks/boat rental
portion of Buckeye Trail (South Fork)

Malabar Farm State Park

For Information

Malabar Farm State Park
Route 1, Box 469
Lucas, OH 44843
(419) 892-2784

Location

Malabar Farm State Park is located about 10 miles southeast of Mansfield on Pleasant Valley Road, just west of S.R. 603. Visitors may also approach S.R. 603 from the south via S.R. 95 from the direction of either Butler or Perrysville. Malabar Farm was the dream of Louis Bromfield, Pulitzer Prize-winning author and dedicated conservationist. In the 1930s he purchased 600 acres of worn-out farmland and, by applying conservation measures, made Malabar productive. Malabar eventually became a showcase for innovative farming practices and Bromfield was visited by agricultural experts from all over the world. In August 1972, the state of Ohio accepted the deed to Malabar Farm; in 1976 Malabar became one of Ohio's state parks. As a park, Malabar Farm is dedicated to perpetuating Bromfield's farming philosophies and providing a place where visitors can explore life on a farm.

Guided tours of the 32-room mansion, known as the Big House, are available daily. Wagon tours are offered on weekends, April 1–October 31, weather permitting. Today, Malabar Farm is still operational. A petting farm is open May 1–October 31. The 914-acre park offers special programs every month; for a calendar of events, contact the park office. There are also larger affairs such as Ohio Heritage Days when more than 100 historic farming and domestic skills are demonstrated. Other annual events include the Sugar Maple Festival and Christmas at Malabar. Malabar Farm's Youth Hostel, administered by the American Youth Hostel organization, offers limited overnight accommodations. For information call: (419) 892-2055.

Facilities & Activities

15 camping sites
youth hostel
15 equestrian campsites
pet camping area
picnicking

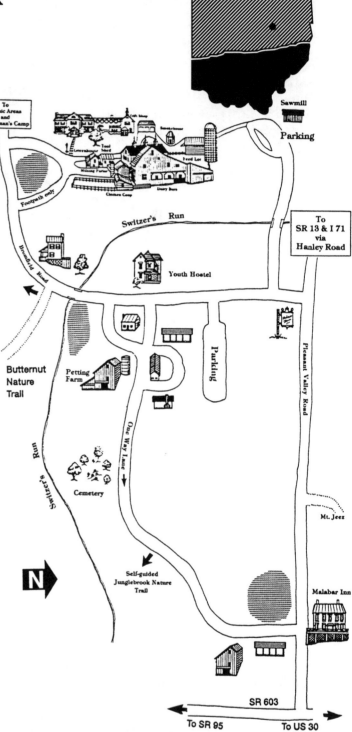

Malabar Inn restaurant (accommodates 60; May 1–October 31)
nature programs
fishing, ice fishing
cross-country skiing/rental
sledding, ice skating
4 miles of hiking trails
12 miles of bridle trails

Maumee Bay State Park

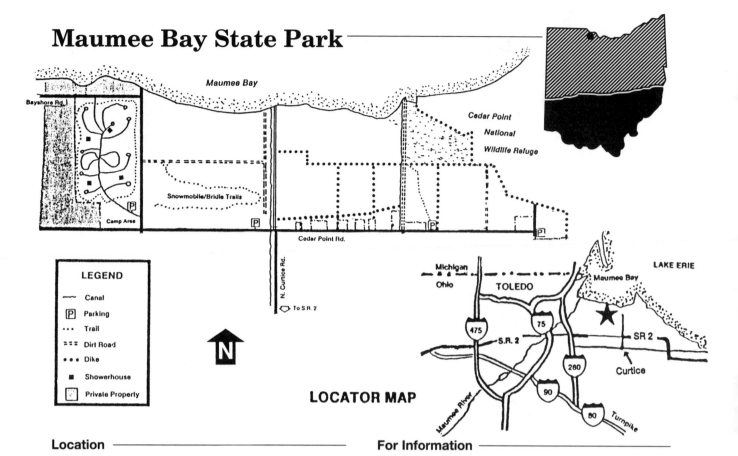

LOCATOR MAP

Location

Maumee Bay State Park is on the shores of Lake Erie's Maumee Bay. To reach the park, travel east of Toledo on S.R. 2 for 8 miles, then 3 miles north on North Curtice Road. This 1,845-acre park offers visitors the opportunity to experience a largely unchanged coastal environment. The marshes of the park are a haven to wildlife, especially waterfowl, during the spring and fall migration periods. The new, modern campground opened during 1981; several sites border ponds, which are open to fishing for campers only. Numerous recreational facilities are planned for the future.

Facilities & Activities

256 camping sites with electricity
showers/flush toilets
dump station
laundry facilities
3 rent-a-camp sites
pet camping area
hunting, fishing, ice fishing
boating (on Lake Erie)
snowmobiling
cross-country skiing
10 miles of hiking trails
8 miles of bridle trails

For Information

Maumee Bay State Park
6505 Cedar Point Road
Oregon, OH 43618
(419) 836-7758

The state park does not have a boat ramp, but Maumee Bay and Lake Erie are ideal for large sailboats.

OHIO REGION 1

Mohawk Lake

For Information

Mohawk Dam
36007 S.R. 715
Warsaw, OH 43844-9534
(614) 824-4343

N

SR 205
Brinkhaven
US 62
Danville
Mohican River
US 62
SR 206
Howard
Millwood
Mohican Wildlife Area
To Mt. Vernon
15 miles
SR 715
Kokosing River
Walhonding
Mohawk Dam
US 62
SR 715
US 36
SR 206
Walhonding River
To Coshocton
12 miles
Newcastle
US 36
Nellie
SR 79
US 36
To Warsaw
3 Miles

Canoe Portage
Trail & Landing
Intake Structure
Walhonding River
Picnic Area
P
Mohawk Dam
SR 715
Stilling Basin
Campground
SR 715
Nature Trails

Location

Mohawk Dam is located northwest of Nellie; U.S. 36 runs parallel to the Kokosing River on the south and S.R. 715 runs parallel on the north. Mohawk is a dry dam, which means the reservoir area does not have a lake throughout the year; this allows maximum storage capacity in the event of a flood. The dam impounds water from the Mohican River and the Kokosing River; the river then becomes the Walhonding River. The campground, operated by the U.S. Army Corps of Engineers, is located near the dam off of S.R. 715. Canoeists enjoy the Walhonding River, suitable for paddlers of all abilities. A mandatory portage is required at Mohawk Dam. The campground is open May–September, specific dates subject to change.

Facilities & Activities

46 campsites (tent or trailer)
  40 fee sites
  6 non-fee sites
flush toilets
water fountains with spigots
playground equipment
2 nature trails
picnic area with grills
fishing
canoeing

The Walhonding River is suitable for paddlers of all abilities; a mandatory portage is required at Mohawk Dam.

Mohican State Park

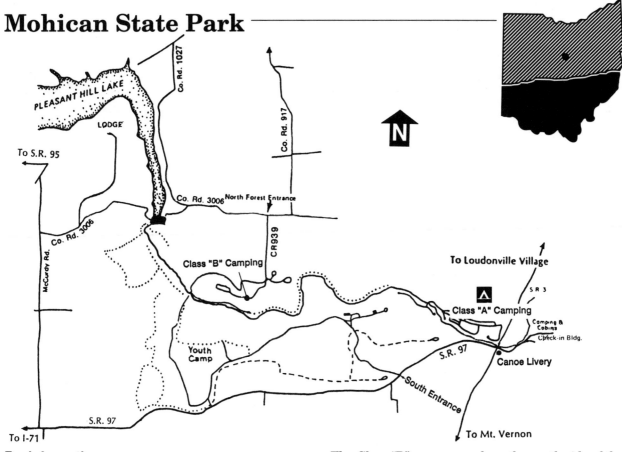

For Information

Mohican State Park
3116 S.R. 3
Loudonville, OH 44842
(419) 994-4290 (camping & cabin reservations)
(419) 938-5411 (lodge)

Location

Mohican State Park is located southwest of Loudonville, off of S.R. 3 and S.R. 97. The 1,294-acre park is adjacent to and surrounded by the larger acreage of the Mohican State Memorial Forest. Both tracts are outstanding in their beauty. The National Park Service has dedicated the Clearfork Gorge area as a Registered National Natural Landmark. The Mohican River, which flows through the park a distance of 5 miles, is one of the finest canoeing rivers in the state. The most popular hiking trail is the 2-mile Lyon's Fall Trail, leading to a waterfall and a sandstone rock shelter; it starts at the covered bridge.

The main campground, off of S.R. 3, is one of Ohio's most popular state park campgrounds; it is the only state park that uses a summer reservation system. Phone the park for a reservation, not more than 4 weeks in advance; a deposit is required.

The Class "B" campground, on the north side of the river nearer the Gorge, is accessible from S.R. 97 via the covered bridge. The lodge and other resort facilities, located on a hill overlooking Pleasant Hill Lake, is accessible from S.R. 97 via McCurdy Road and C. R. 3006.

Facilities & Activities

177 camping sites
   153 sites with electricity
showers/flush toilets
dump station
laundry facilities
camp commissary
group camp (100 capacity)
25 family housekeeping cabins
96-room resort lodge
   restaurant
   indoor & outdoor pools
   tennis
picnicking, 4 picnic shelters
summer nature programs
fishing
canoeing/canoe rentals
tubing
9 miles of hiking trails

Mosquito Lake State Park

Mosquito Lake is one of Ohio's largest lakes.

N

For Information

Mosquito Lake State Park
1439 S.R. 305
Cortland, OH 44410
(216) 637-2856
(216) 638-5700 (camp office)

Location

Mosquito Lake State Park is located 10 miles northeast of Warren off of S.R. 46 and S.R. 305. The office and campground for this 3,961-acre park are located off of S.R. 305 along the southwest shore. Mosquito Lake, with a summer pool of 7,850 acres, is one of the largest lakes in Ohio; it provides endless opportunities for water enthusiasts. The 9.6-mile long lake is unique in that it has an uncontrolled natural spillway. Normally, the water flows south through the dam to the Mahoning Valley. But when the lake fills to the elevation of 904 feet above sea level, the flow reverses and the natural spillway is used. The outlet is located at the north end of the lake and water flowing in that direction reaches a tributary of Grand River, then the Grand River itself and eventually Lake Erie.

Facilities & Activities

234 camping sites
showers
dump station
boat dock/tie-ups at campground
picnicking
600-foot swimming beach
hunting, fishing, ice fishing
boating/water skiing
4 boat ramps
boat rental/seasonal dock rental
boat fuel
snowmobiling
cross-country skiing
sledding, ice skating
2 miles of hiking trails

Mount Gilead State Park

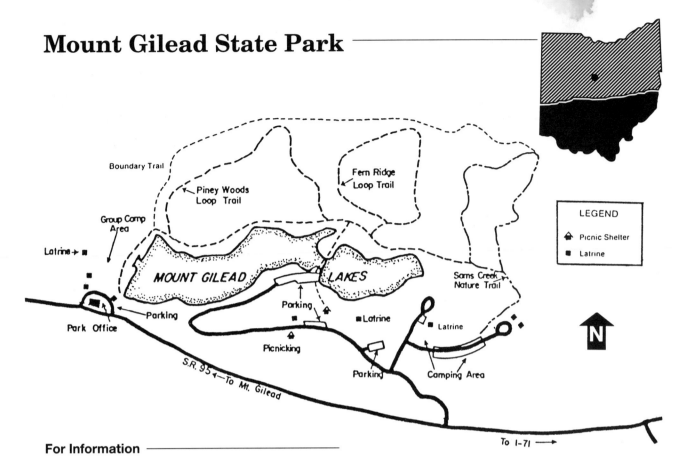

For Information

Mount Gilead State Park
4119 S.R. 95
Mt. Gilead, OH 43338
(419) 946-1961

Location

Mount Gilead State Park is located 1 mile east of Mt. Gilead on S.R. 95. The campground at this 40-acre park affords large shaded sites in a pine and hardwood forest. The park has 2 lakes, totaling 32 acres; both provide good fishing for catfish, bluegill, and crappie. Canoeing and rowboating are popular boating pastimes. Three hiking trails explore the park's mature woodlands.

Facilities & Activities

60 camping sites
dump station
4 rent-a-camp sites
group camp (120 capacity)
picnicking, picnic shelter
fishing, ice fishing
boating (electric motors only)
boat ramp
sledding, ice skating
3 miles of hiking trails

An angler tries his luck below the dam between the two small lakes.

North Branch of Kokosing River Lake

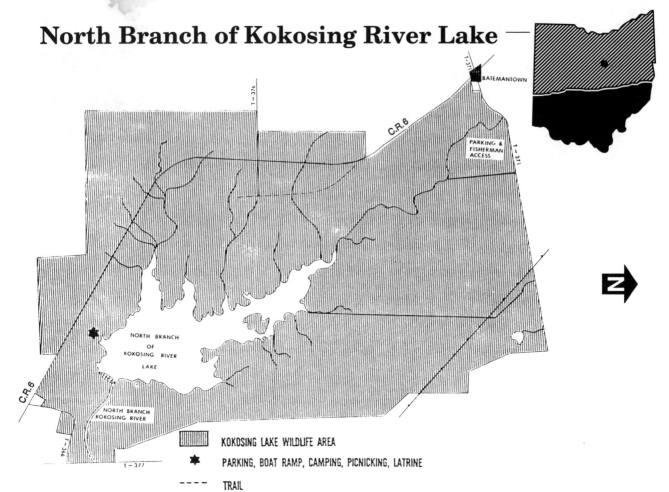

KOKOSING LAKE WILDLIFE AREA

★ PARKING, BOAT RAMP, CAMPING, PICNICKING, LATRINE

- - - - TRAIL

For Information

North Branch of Kokosing River Lake
Route 2
Fredericktown, OH 43019

Location

North Branch of Kokosing River Lake is located
2 miles northwest of Fredericktown via C.R. 6

*Much to the delight of children, playground equipment
is provided at many of the parks.*

(Waterford Road) and 5 miles northeast of Chester-
ville. The lake is part of the flood control system for
the Muskingum River basin. The spillway is a part
of the earthfill dam structure that allows high
water to bypass the dam instead of damaging it by
going over the top. The minimum year-round storage is 154 surface acres; the maximum pool level
for flood control storage is 1,146 surface acres. The
campground, operated by the U.S. Army Corps of
Engineers, is located off of C.R. 6 on the south side
of the lake. The campground is open May–September; specific dates subject to change. The picnic area and launch ramp are open year-round.

Facilities & Activities

42 campsites
   36 fee sites
   6 non-fee sites
vault toilets
water fountains with spigots
playground equipment
picnic area
boating (10 h.p. motor limit)
boat ramp

Piedmont Lake

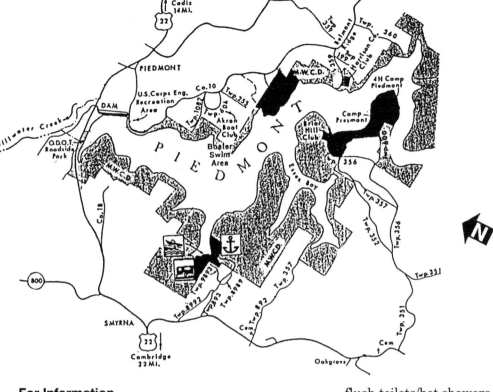

For Information

Piedmont Lake Marina
Route 1
Piedmont, OH 43983
(614) 658-3735

Location

Piedmont Lake is south of U.S. 22, which runs between Smyrna and Piedmont. S.R. 800 from Smyrna is west of the lake and S.R. 331 from Piedmont is east of the lake. From the south, S.R. 800 is accessible from I-70, exit 202, at Hendrysburg. The lake has a surface area of 2,270 acres and a land area totaling 4,372 acres. A campground is located at the marina on a cove along the northwest shore; it is accessible via a paved road from S.R. 800, just south of its junction with U.S. 22. The campground and marina are open from April 1 through November 1. Pets are permitted in designated areas.

Facilities & Activities

87 campsites
  16 full hookups
  71 electric only
flush toilets/hot showers
dump station
motel
picnic area
playground
hunting, fishing
boating (10 h.p. maximum)
marina/supplies/lunch counter
boat ramp/docks/rental
portion of Buckeye Trail

Many anglers seem to prefer shoreline fishing over fishing from a boat.

Pleasant Hill Lake

For Information

Pleasant Hill Lake Park
Route 2, Box 131
Perrysville, OH 44864
(419) 938-7884

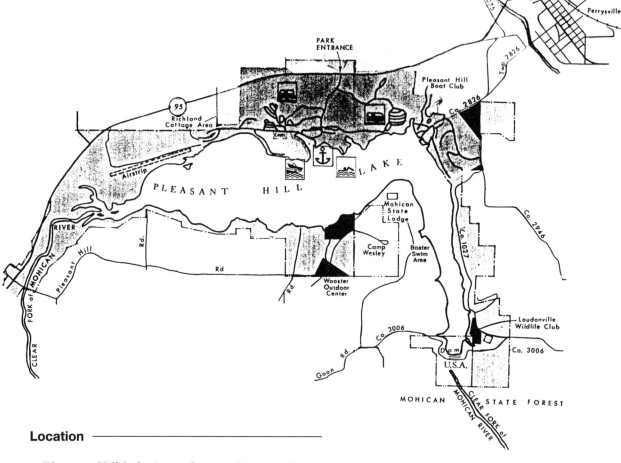

Location

Pleasant Hill Lake is southwest of Perrysville off of S.R. 95. The 850-acre lake, with 13 miles of shoreline, and 1,345-acre land area is adjacent to Clearfork Gorge and the Mohican Memorial State Forest. The Mohican State Park Lodge overlooks the lake from a hill along the southeast shoreline. The Pleasant Hill Lake Park is located on the north side of the lake off of S.R. 95; the campground and full-service marina are within the park, along with numerous other facilities. The park is open year-round. Pets are permitted in designated area.

Facilities & Activities

426 campsites
electric hookups
flush toilets/hot showers
vacation cabins (sleep 6)
camper cabins
group camping
picnic area/grills
group shelter
playground
swimming beach, concession stand
nature/hiking trails
amphitheater
airstrip
hunting, fishing
boating/waterskiing
marina/supplies/lunch counter
boat ramp/docks/rentals

Portage Lakes State Park

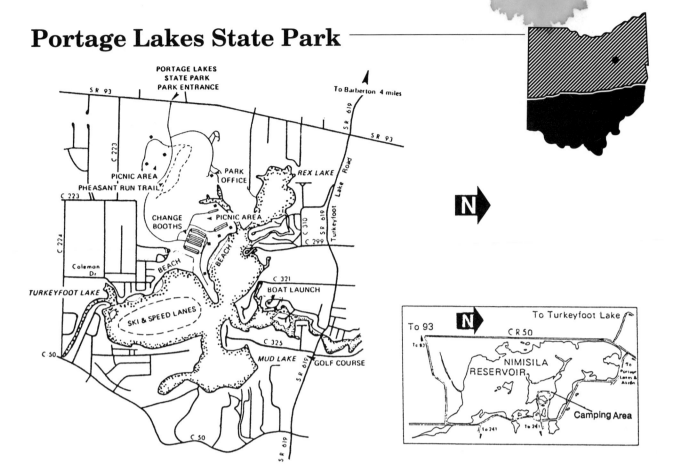

For Information

Portage Lakes State Park
5031 Manchester Road
Akron, OH 44319-3999
(216) 644-2220

Location

The entrance to Portage Lakes State Park is located 10 miles south of Akron, 2 miles south of S.R. 619, on S.R. 93. Portage Lakes acquired their name from their proximity to the historically famous portage trail between the Cuyahoga and Tuscarawas rivers the Indians used for centuries. The 8-mile trail was the only land the Indians had to portage while canoeing from Lake Erie to the Ohio River. The park consists of 450 acres of land and 2,520 acres of water. Ski and speed zones are marked by buoys on East Reservoir and Turkeyfoot Lake; these zones have specific hours for activity. Other lakes are no-wake zones; sailing is popular at Nimisila Reservoir. A public boat launching ramp is located near the lake patrol office, about 2 miles east of S.R. 93 off of S.R. 619.

The park office, swimming beach and picnic area are located on the west side of Turkeyfoot Lake off of S.R. 93. The campground is on the east side of Nimisila Reservoir, accessible via East Nimisila Road. If approaching from the east on I-77, take exit 120 and travel south on Arlington Road, then west on East Nimisila Road. If approaching from the west on S.R. 93, turn east on S.R. 619, then south on Arlington Road and west on East Nimisila Road.

Facilities & Activities

104 camping sites (Nimisila Reservoir)
dump station
pet camping area
picnicking, picnic shelter
900-foot swimming beach (Turkeyfoot Lake)
hunting, fishing, ice fishing
boating/water skiing (Turkeyfoot Lake & East Reservoir)
boating (electric motors only at Nimisila Reservoir)
no-wake boating on other lakes
boat ramp
snowmobiling
ice skating
5 miles of hiking trails

Punderson State Park

For Information

Punderson State Park
Box 338, 11755 Kinsman Road
Newbury, OH 44065
(216) 564-1195 (camp office)
(216) 564-9144 (lodge)

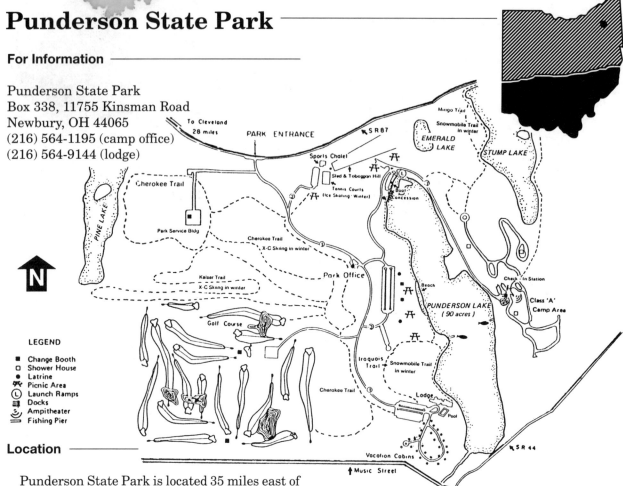

Location

Punderson State Park is located 35 miles east of Cleveland on S.R. 87, 2 miles east of S.R. 44. Punderson Lake, the largest and deepest of Ohio's glacial lakes, is the focal point of the many land and water-based recreational opportunities at this 846-acre park. Two smaller fishing lakes bring the total water acres at the park to 150. The land was once owned by Lemuel Punderson who operated a grist mill and distillery here. In 1929 work began on a Tudor-style manor but was never completed. After the state purchased the land and incomplete house, a park was opened in 1951. In 1956 the completely remodeled Manor House opened to the public to become one of Ohio's first state park lodges. A major structural renovation of the Manor House was completed in 1982. Punderson has become Ohio's premier winter sports park. Winter activities center around the unique winter sports chalet that sits atop the large sledding hill and offers enthusiasts a warming fire and refreshments.

Facilities & Activities

201 camping sites with electricity
showers/flush toilets
dump station
laundry facilities
4 rent-a-camp sites
26 family housekeeping cabins
31-room resort lodge
   restaurant
   outdoor pool
   tennis
   18-hole golf course
pet camping area
picnicking
summer nature programs
600-foot swimming beach
fishing, ice fishing
boating (electric motors only)
boat ramp/rental/seasonal dock rental
food service
snowmobiling
cross-country skiing/rentals
sled & tobaggon run/rentals
ice skating
8½ miles of hiking trails

Pymatuning State Park

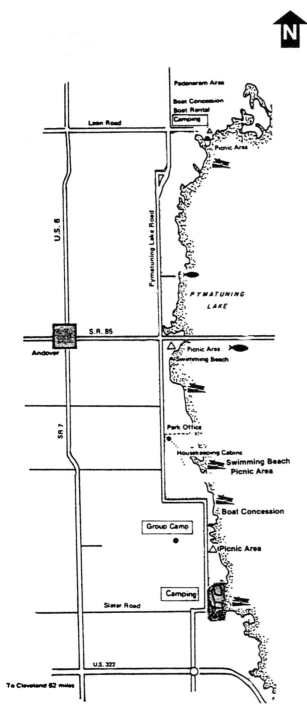

LEGEND

☐ Washhouse

▨ Playground

⊟ Launch Ramp

⬭ Fishing Access

Location

Pymatuning State Park is located 2 miles east of Andover on S.R. 85. The park's recreational facilities are located along the western shore of the 14,000-acre Pymatuning Lake off of Pymatuning Lake Road. The park office is on Pymatuning Lake Road south of S.R. 85; the cabins are nearby. Continue south on Pymatuning Lake Road to reach the campground. The campground can also be reached by traveling south on S.R. 7, then east on Slater Road. The small primitive campground is north of S.R. 85. The reservoir has a reputation as one of the finest fishing lakes in Ohio. Because of its location in the "snow belt," this 3,500-acre park also enjoys the reputation as one of the most popular parks for winter recreation.

Facilities & Activities

373 camping sites
   352 sites with electricity
showers/flush toilets
dump station
laundry facilities
camp commissary
150-foot beach at campground
boat dock/tie-ups at campground
boat launch at campground
group camp (400 capacity)
27 family housekeeping cabins
35 standard housekeeping cabins (4/1–10/31)
10 primitive walk-in campsites
picnicking, 3 picnic shelters
summer nature programs
350-foot swimming beach
beach concession
hunting, fishing, ice fishing
boating (10-h.p. limit)
5 boat ramps
boat rental
cross-country skiing
ice skating, ice boating
3 miles of hiking trails

For Information

Pymatuning State Park
Route 1
Andover, OH 44003
(216) 293-6329
(216) 293-6684 (camp office)

Salt Fork State Park

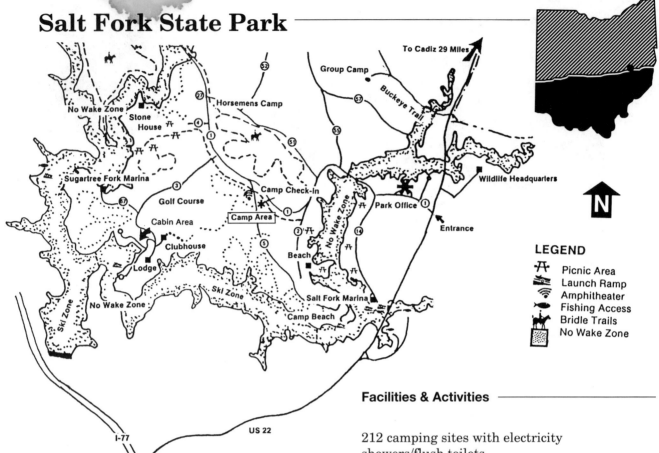

Facilities & Activities

212 camping sites with electricity
showers/flush toilets
dump station
beach at campground
boat dock/tie-ups at campground
boat launch at campground
group camp (100 capacity)
25 equestrian camp sites
54 family housekeeping cabins
148-room resort lodge
   restaurant
   indoor pool & outdoor pool
   tennis
   18-hole golf course
pet camping area
picnicking, picnic shelter
summer nature programs
2,500-foot swimming beach
beach concession
hunting, fishing, ice fishing
boating/water skiing
6 boat ramps
boat rental/seasonal dock rental
boat fuel/food service
snowmobiling, ice boating
cross-country skiing
sledding, ice skating
14 miles of hiking trails
25 miles of bridle trails

For Information

Salt Fork State Park
P.O. Box 672, S.R. 22 E.
Cambridge, OH 43725-0672
(614) 439-3521
(614) 439-2751 (lodge)

Location

Salt Fork State Park is located 8 miles northeast of Cambridge off of U.S. 22; if traveling on I-77, take exit 47 and travel east. Boasting 17,229 land acres and a 2,952-acre lake, Salt Fork is Ohio's largest state park. The beautiful countryside of southeastern Ohio encouraged the development of extensive recreation facilities around the reservoir, originally slated only as a water source for the city of Cambridge. Access to the park's facilities are past the park office via the park entrance off of U.S. 22. The lodge, scenically located on a peninsula stretching into the lake, has all the features of a fine resort. The park is popular for year-round activities; special thrills await the hardy visitor in the winter.

South Bass Island State Park

For Information

South Bass Island State Park
4049 E. Moores Dock Road
Port Clinton, OH 43452
(419) 797-4530

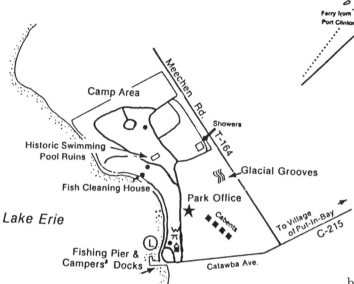

Location

South Bass Island State Park is located on one of the most historic islands in the western Lake Erie basin. It was in the waters near South Bass Island that the famous Battle of Lake Erie was fought during the War of 1812. Perry's Victory and International Peace Memorial commemorates the battle; the 352-foot monument is the third tallest monument in the U.S. It is located on a 25-acre tract and overlooks Put-in-Bay. Ferry service to South Bass is available from Catawba and Port Clinton. The 35-acre state park is located on the southwest corner of the island at the end of Catawba Avenue (C.R. 215). The campsites are in a shady grove overlooking Lake Erie. Bicycle touring is popular on South Bass Island, especially during the summer months. An island taxi service is available as well.

Facilities & Activities

135 camping sites
showers
dump station
boat dock/tie-ups at campground
4 cabents (Memorial Day–October 1)
picnicking, picnic shelter
summer nature programs
small stone beach
bicycling
fishing, ice fishing
fish cleaning house
boating on Lake Erie
boat ramp

The state park on South Bass Island is located on the southwest corner of the island.

Tappan Lake

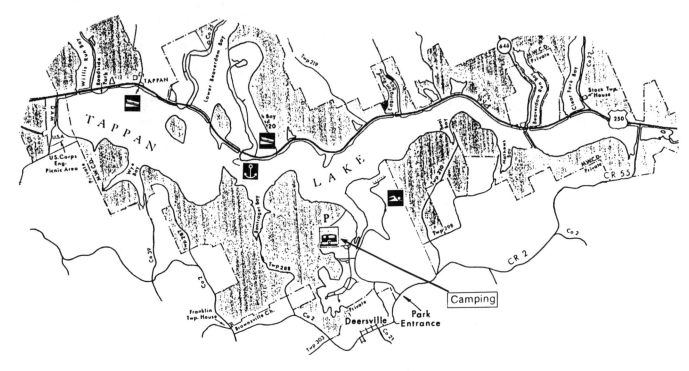

For Information

Tappan Lake Park
Box 29
Deersville, OH 44693
(614) 922-3649

Location

Tappan Lake is along U.S. 250 that runs between Uhrichsville and Cadiz; in fact, the highway is along the north shore the entire length of the lake. Tappan Lake, built for flood control, has 2,350 surface acres and a land area of 5,026 acres. A full-service marina is just off of U.S. 250 on North Bay Road. The campground is at Tappan Lake Park, north of Deersville; it is accessible from U.S. 250 at the east end of the lake; take C.R. 55 (Deersville Road), then C.R. 2 to the park entrance. The park is a full facility outdoor recreation center and is open year-round. Pets are permitted in designated areas.

Facilities & Activities

500 campsites
electric hookups at all sites
flush toilets/hot showers
group camping
vacation cabins (sleep 6; 1 sleeps 8)
camper cabins
picnic area/grills
group shelter
playground
miniature golf course
swimming beach
concession stand
activity center/nature center
amphitheater
hiking trails
hunting, fishing
boating/waterskiing (120 h.p. maximum)
marina/supplies (on U.S. 250)
    restaurant/lunch counter
    boat ramp/docks/rentals
    fishing cabins

Van Buren State Park

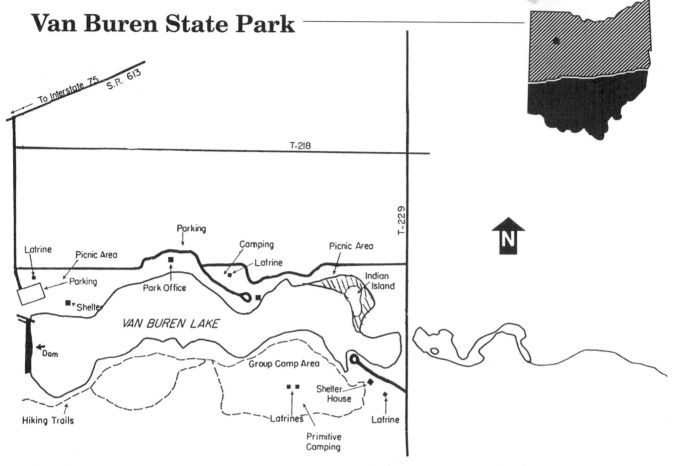

For Information

Van Buren State Park
12259 Twp. Road 218
Van Buren, OH 45889
(419) 299-3461

Location

Van Buren State Park is located southeast of Van Buren; from exit 164 on I-75, travel east on S.R. 613 beyond Van Buren, then south. The area that is now Van Buren State Park was originally inhabited by the Shawnee Indians. The woodlands of this 238-acre park are a small but valued refuge in the rich agricultural lands of northwestern Ohio. It was established as a state park in 1950. The 60-acre lake was formed by building a dam across Rocky Ford Creek.

Van Buren Lake was formed by building a dam across Rocky Ford Creek.

Facilities & Activities

48 camping sites
dump station
youth group camp (200 capacity; walk-in sites; tents only)
pet camping area

picnicking, picnic shelter
hunting, fishing, ice fishing
boating (electric motors only)
5 miles of hiking trails
2 miles of bridle trails

West Branch State Park

For Information

West Branch State Park
5708 Esworthy Road
Route 5
Ravenna, OH 44266-9659
(216) 296-3239

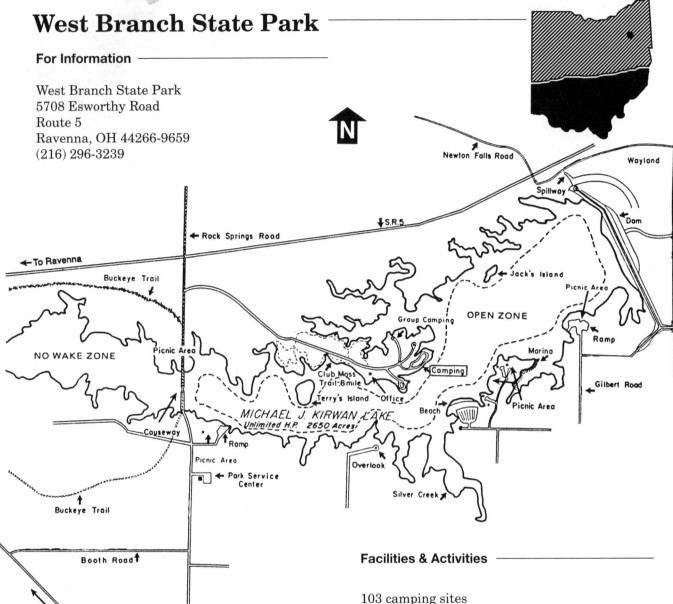

Location

West Branch State Park is located 4 miles east of Ravenna off of S.R. 5; if traveling on I-80, south of the lake, take exit 43 onto S.R. 14 and travel northwest toward Ravenna. Access to the various facilities in the park is possible from a number of well-posted roads off of the main roads. The park office and campground to this 5,352-acre park are on the north side of the lake off of Rock Springs Road. West Branch is extremely popular among fishermen and boaters. The 2,650-acre lake is about 10 miles long and with its many forks and coves offers about 36 miles of shoreline.

Facilities & Activities

103 camping sites
dump station
5 rent-a-camp sites
group camp (100 capacity)
picnicking, picnic shelters
nature center
summer nature programs
1,100-foot swimming beach
beach concession
hunting, fishing, ice fishing
boating/water skiing
boat ramps/rental/seasonal dock rental
boat fuel/food service
snowmobiling
cross-country skiing
sledding, ice skating
3.4 miles of hiking trails
4-mile portion of Buckeye Trail
20 miles of bridle trails

Ohio Region 2

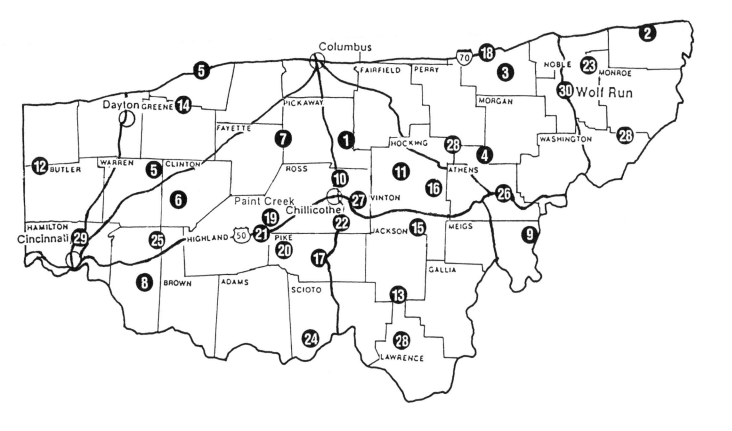

A. W. Marion State Park

For Information

A. W. Marion State Park
7317 Warner-Huffer Road
Circleville, OH 43113
(614) 474-3386

Location

A.W. Marion State Park is located 4 miles northeast of Circleville off U.S. 22 or S.R. 188. The 308-acre park is located in the roughest terrain in Pickaway County, known as "The Devil's Backbone." In 1962, the park was renamed the A.W. Marion State Park in honor of the first director of the Department of Natural Resources, a Pickaway County native. The campground is located on the east side of the park's 146-acre lake and is accessible via East Ringgold-Southern Road. The park office and the A.W. Marion Memorial are located on the west side of the lake in the day-use area, accessible via Bolender Road.

Facilities & Activities

60 camping sites
dump station
group camp (160 capacity; walk-in sites; tents only)
pet camping area
picnicking
hunting, fishing, ice fishing
boating (electric motors only)
boat ramp/rental/food service
sledding, ice skating
6 miles of hiking trails

Good catches of panfish, bass, muskellunge, and catfish are taken from Hargus Lake.

Barkcamp State Park

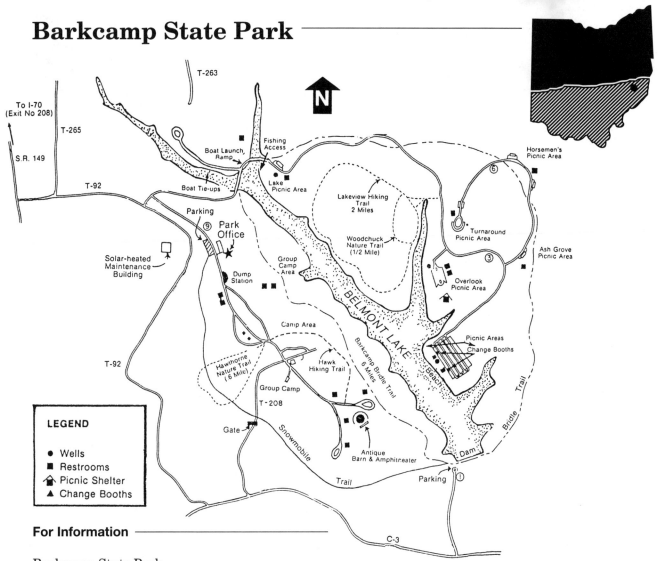

For Information

Barkcamp State Park
65330 Barkcamp Park Road
Belmont, OH 43718
(614) 484-4064

Location

    Barkcamp State Park is located 1 mile south of I-70, exit 208, off of S.R. 149. Three major streams and numerous creeks course through the rolling terrain of this 1,115-acre park. The land varies from mature forest to open meadows and supports abundant wildlife. The park derives its unusual name from Barkcamp Creek, the former site of a logging operation at which logs were stripped of their bark in preparation for delivery to a mill. The park's 117-acre lake resulted from impounding Barkcamp Creek. The park office, campground, and an "antique barn" are located on the west side of the lake; the barn offers visitors a brief journey into Ohio's rural past.

Facilities & Activities

151 camping sites
showers
dump station
boat dock/tie-ups at campground
4 rent-a-camp sites
group camp (150 capacity)
pet camping area
picnicking, picnic shelter
nature center
summer nature programs
700-foot swimming beach
beach concession
hunting, fishing
boating (electric motors only)
boat ramp/rental/food service
snowmobiling
4 miles of hiking trails
9 miles of bridle trails

Blue Rock State Park

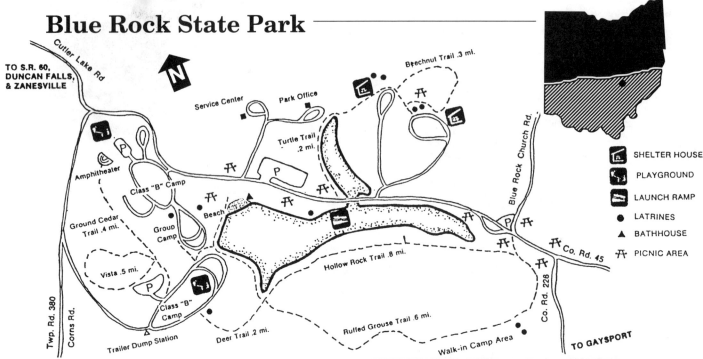

SHELTER HOUSE
PLAYGROUND
LAUNCH RAMP
• LATRINES
▲ BATHHOUSE
PICNIC AREA

For Information

Blue Rock State Park
7924 Cutler Lake Road
Blue Rock, OH 43720
(614) 674-4794

Location

Blue Rock State Park is located 15 miles southeast of Zanesville. The main entrance is on C.R. 45 (Cutler Lake Road), 6 miles from S.R. 60. The park office is off Park Road 3, opposite the beach area. This 335-acre park, originally part of Blue Rock State Forest, is adjacent to and in the southernmost portion of the 4,573-acre state forest. The name "Blue Rock" is derived from the outcrops of shale along the Muskingum River, which actually appear to be blue, particularly when it is wet from overhead springs or rainfall. The 15-acre lake is ideal for canoes, rowboats, and boats with electric motors.

Visitors to Ohio state parks are greeted with attractive entrance signs; some are more elaborate than others.

Facilities & Activities

101 camping sites
showers
dump station
3 rent-a-camp sites
youth group camp (128 capacity)
20 primitive campsites
pet camping area

picnicking, picnic shelter
swimming beach
fishing, ice fishing
boating (electric motors only)
boat ramps
ice skating
ice boating
3 miles of hiking trails

Burr Oak State Park

For Information

Burr Oak State Park
Route 2, Box 286
Glouster, OH 45732
(614) 767-3683 (camp office)
(614) 767-2112 (lodge)

Legend:
▲ Latrine
〰 Docks or Tie-ups
·))) Amphitheater
ⓒ Park roads
— Buckeye Trail
--- Burr Oak Backpack Trail
★ Backpack Camp Area

Location

Burr Oak State Park is located northeast of Glouster off of S.R. 13 & 78. The 2,592-acre park is one of Ohio's 7 resort parks and offers a wide array of overnight accommodations. The 664-acre Burr Oak Lake was created by the construction of the Jenkins Dam across Sunday Creek. The lake offers water sports enthusiasts numerous recreational opportunities. The park office, public beach, and the Class A campground are on the west side of the lake, accessible from S.R. 13, while the lodge and cabins are east of the lake and accessible from S.R. 78.

Facilities & Activities

100 camping sites
showers/flush toilets
dump station
laundry facilities
boat dock/tie-ups at campground
3 rent-a-camp sites
30 family housekeeping cabins
60-room resort lodge
   restaurant
   indoor/outdoor pool
   tennis
3 backpack camp areas
picnicking
nature center, summer nature programs
swimming beach
beach concession
hunting, fishing, ice fishing
boating (10-h.p. limit)
4 boat ramps
boat fuel/rental/seasonal dock rental
cross-country skiing, sledding
10 miles of hiking trails
29 miles of backpacking trails (portion of Buckeye Trail)
8 miles of bridle trails

Caesar Creek State Park

For Information

Caesar Creek State Park
8570 East S.R. 73
Waynesville, OH 45068
(513) 897-3055
(513) 488-4595 (camp office)

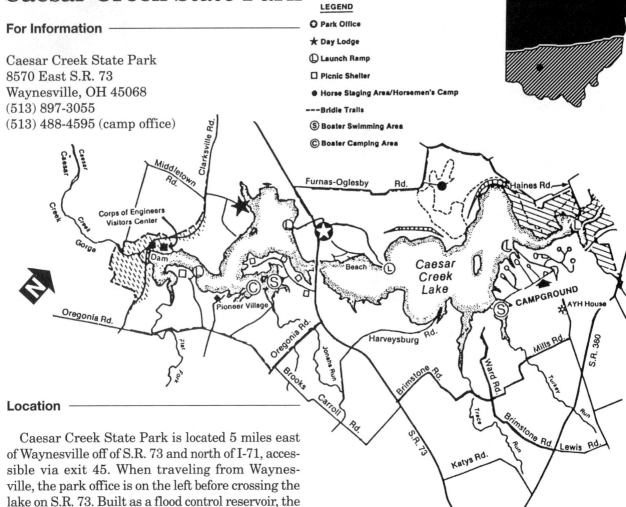

LEGEND

- ✪ Park Office
- ★ Day Lodge
- Ⓛ Launch Ramp
- ☐ Picnic Shelter
- ● Horse Staging Area/Horsemen's Camp
- --- Bridle Trails
- Ⓢ Boater Swimming Area
- Ⓒ Boater Camping Area

Location

Caesar Creek State Park is located 5 miles east of Waynesville off of S.R. 73 and north of I-71, accessible via exit 45. When traveling from Waynesville, the park office is on the left before crossing the lake on S.R. 73. Built as a flood control reservoir, the crystal blue waters of the 2,830-acre Caesar Creek Lake offer some of the finest boating and fishing in Ohio. The 7,941 acres of gently rolling terrain support miles of bridle, backpack, snowmobile, and cross-country ski trails. The campground is on Center Road, accessible from S.R. 380 or from S.R. 73, via Brimstone Road and Mills Road. One of the focal points at Caesar Creek is the Pioneer Village where many examples of early log architecture have been restored and preserved by a private historical society. The village is open year-round for self-guided tours.

Facilities & Activities

287 camping sites with electricity
showers/flush toilets
dump station
boat launch at campground
4 rent-a-camp sites
horsemen's camp sites (30 individual; 15 group)
pet camping area
picnicking, 5 picnic shelters
summer nature programs
1,300-foot swimming beach
beach concession
hunting, fishing, ice fishing
boating/water skiing
5 boat ramps/seasonal dock rental
snowmobiling
cross-country skiing
ice skating
32 miles of hiking trails
50 miles of backpacking trails (portion of Buckeye Trail)
25 miles of bridle trails

Cowan Lake State Park

For Information

Cowan Lake State Park
729 Beechwood Road
Wilmington, OH 45177
(513) 289-2105

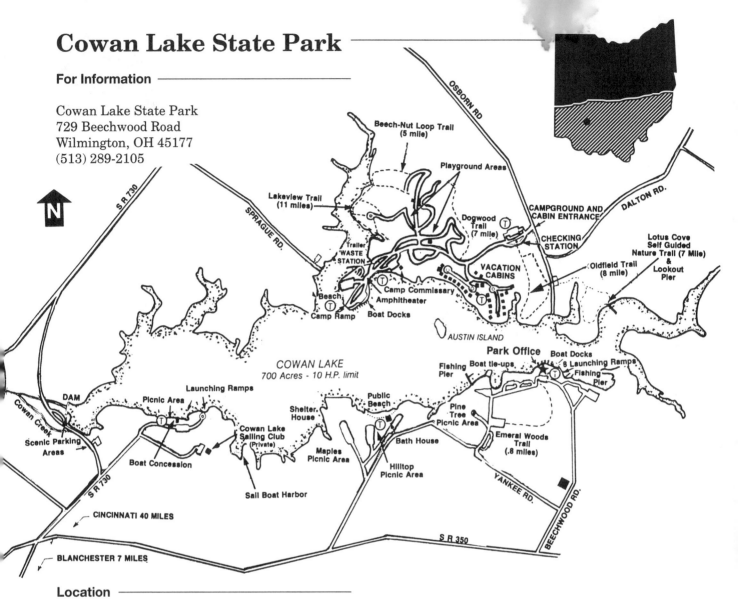

Location

Cowan Lake State Park is located 5 miles southwest of Wilmington and bounded on the east by U.S. 68 and on the west by S.R. 730. The 700-acre lake is considered one of the finest sailing lakes in the midwest. The park office and the day-use facilities are on the south side of the lake, accessible via S.R. 350. The overnight accommodations for this 1,075-acre park are on the north side of the lake. Cowan Lake boasts several fine hiking trails. The Lotus Cove self-guided trail provides a boardwalk view of an American lotus (water lily) colony, one of the most spectacular of Ohio's water plants.

Facilities & Activities

237 camping sites with electricity
27 family housekeeping cabins
showers/flush toilets
dump station
laundry facilities
camp commissary
beach at campground
boat dock/tie-ups at campground
boat launch at campground
pet camping area
picnicking, picnic shelter
summer nature programs
1,000-foot swimming beach
beach concession
hunting, fishing, ice fishing
boating (10-h.p. limit)
5 boat ramps
boat rental/seasonal dock rental
boat fuel/food service
sledding
4½ miles of hiking trails

Deer Creek State Park

For Information

Deer Creek State Park
20635 Waterloo Road
Mt. Sterling, OH 43143
(614) 869-3508 (camp office)
(614) 869-2020 (lodge/cabins)

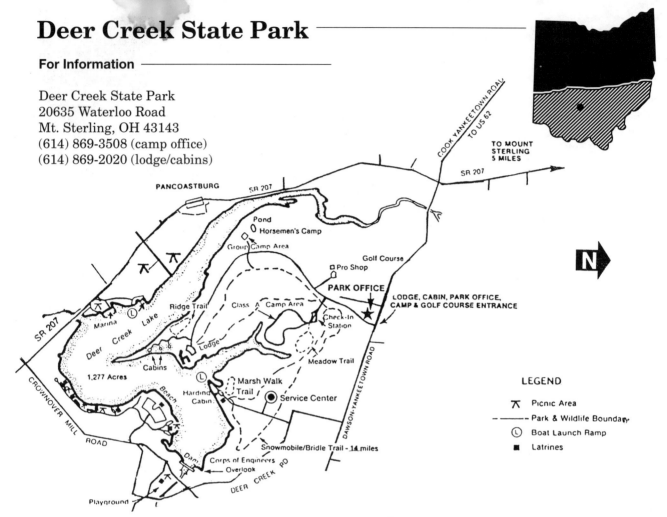

Location

Deer Creek State Park is located south of Mount Sterling on S.R. 207. The 6,348-acre park is Ohio's newest resort park; attracting the most attention is its full-facility lodge and cabin complex. These facilities, as well as the park office, campground, and golf course are reached by traveling east on Dawson-Yankeetown Road from S.R. 207. The 1,277-acre lake offers water recreation of every description. Biking on the level park roads is also a favorite pastime. A rustic one and a half story cabin built in 1918 overlooks the valley; it was the historic retreat of President Harding and is available for rental.

Facilities & Activities

232 camping sites with electricity
showers/flush toilets
dump station
4 rent-a-camp sites
youth group camp (100 capacity; walk-in sites; tents only)
3 equestrian campsites
25 family housekeeping cabins
3-bedroom Harding Cabin
110-room resort lodge
  restaurant
  indoor/outdoor pools
  tennis
  18-hole golf course
pet camping area
picnicking
summer nature programs
1,700-foot swimming beach
beach concession
hunting, fishing, ice fishing
boating/water skiing
2 boat ramps
boat rental/seasonal dock rental
boat fuel/food service
snowmobiling
ice skating
5 miles of hiking trails
14 miles of bridle trails

East Fork State Park

For Information

East Fork State Park
Box 119
Bethel, OH 45106
(513) 734-4323
(513) 724-6521 (camp office)

Location

East Fork State Park is situated in the Little Miami River Basin northwest of Bethel and southwest of Williamsburg. The 8,420-acre park, one of Ohio's largest state parks, includes both rugged hills and open meadows. Access to the park's main recreational opportunities are from S.R. 32 and S.R. 125. The park office and the public beach are on the south side of the 2,160-acre lake, just north of S.R. 125; the campground is on the north side of the lake, accessible from S.R. 32. An extensive trail system encircles the lake. East Fork Lake is also known as William H. Harsha Lake.

Facilities & Activities

416 camping sites with electricity
showers/flush toilets
dump station
beach at campground
boat launch at campground
4 rent-a-camp sites
17 equestrian campsites
4 overnight areas on the backcountry trail
pet camping area
picnicking, picnic shelter
summer nature programs
1,200-foot swimming beach
beach concession
hunting, fishing, ice fishing
boating/water skiing
5 boat ramps
sledding, ice skating
12-mile backpack trail (south side)
33-mile hiking/bridle backcountry trail (perimeter)
other bridle trail loops (north side)
8-mile portion of Buckeye Trail

Forked Run State Park

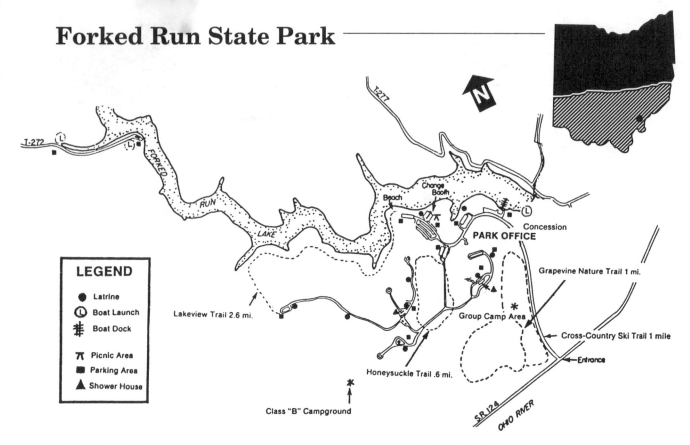

LEGEND

- ● Latrine
- Ⓛ Boat Launch
- 🎋 Boat Dock
- 🕇 Picnic Area
- ■ Parking Area
- ▲ Shower House

Lakeview Trail 2.6 mi.

Grapevine Nature Trail 1 mi.

Cross-Country Ski Trail 1 mile

Entrance

Group Camp Area

Honeysuckle Trail .6 mi.

Class "B" Campground

Concession

PARK OFFICE

Beach

Change Booth

S.R. 124

OHIO RIVER

For Information

Forked Run State Park
S.R. 124
Reedsville, OH 45772
(614) 378-6206

Location

Forked Run State Park is located on S.R. 124 southwest of Reedsville, just north of the Ohio River. The park office, campground and all of the recreational facilities are located on the south side of Forked Run Lake. The park is adjacent to the 2,562-acre Shade River State Forest. The camp-ground, situated on the hilltops overlooking a scenic valley, offers easy access to the 102-acre lake. Three hiking trails are located in the 715-acre park and offer the hiker a chance to explore the rugged forest terrain.

Facilities & Activities

198 camping sites
showers
dump station
laundry facilities
boat dock/tie-ups at campground
3 rent-a-camp sites
group camp (120 capacity)
pet camping area
picnicking
500-foot swimming beach
hunting, fishing, ice fishing
boating (10-h.p. limit)
2 boat ramps/boat rental
cross-country skiing
sledding, ice skating
4 miles of hiking trails

The campground at Forked Run offers a relaxed atmosphere; shaded and open sites are available.

Great Seal State Park

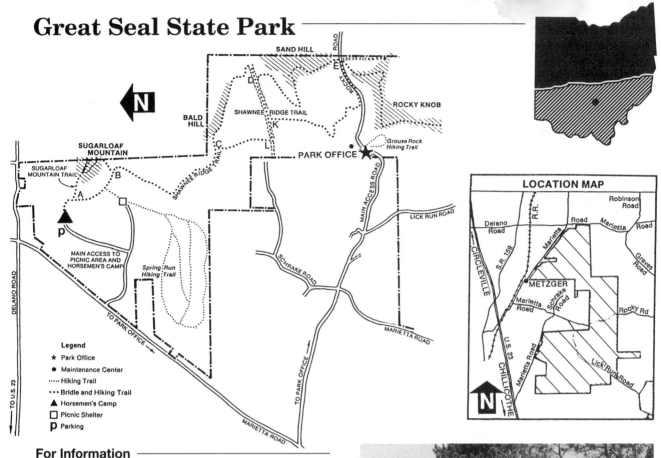

For Information

Great Seal State Park
825 Rocky Road
Chillicothe, OH 45601
(614) 773-2726

Location

Great Seal State Park, one of Ohio's newest recreational areas, is located 5 miles northeast of Chillicothe on Marietta Road. The park got its name from the state emblem—The Great Seal of Ohio. The famous scene, depicting a sun suspended over rolling hills and shocked wheat, was inspired by these very hills. William Creighton, an early secretary of state, is credited with designing the seal. The 1,864-acre park is dedicated to the wilderness spirit of early Ohio.

Twenty miles of trails are available to both hikers and equestrians; the terrain varies from steep to gently rolling. It is advised that horses and hikers be well conditioned for these trails; there is limited water in streams for horses. The primitive equestrian camp, located in the northern portion of the park off Marietta Road, is the only campground. The park has 2 trails that are strictly footpaths: the Spring Run Trail starts at the picnic area near the

The park has 17 miles of bridle trails; the terrain varies from steep to gently rolling.

campground and the Grouse Rock Trail starts at the park office. During the winter months, the Spring Run Trail is available for cross-country skiers.

Facilities & Activities

15 equestrian campsites
pet camping area
picnicking, picnic shelter
hunting
cross-country skiing
21 miles of hiking trails
17 miles of bridle trails

Hocking Hills State Park

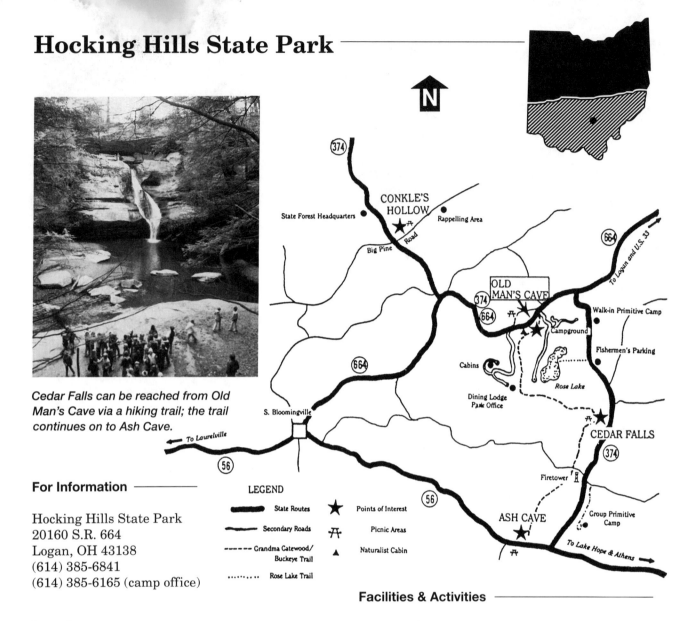

Cedar Falls can be reached from Old Man's Cave via a hiking trail; the trail continues on to Ash Cave.

LEGEND

▬▬▬ State Routes	★ Points of Interest
━━━ Secondary Roads	⛼ Picnic Areas
----- Grandma Gatewood/ Buckeye Trail	▲ Naturalist Cabin
·········· Rose Lake Trail	

For Information

Hocking Hills State Park
20160 S.R. 664
Logan, OH 43138
(614) 385-6841
(614) 385-6165 (camp office)

Location

Hocking Hills State Park is located 50 miles southeast of Columbus off of U.S. 33. The 2,331-acre Hocking Hills complex is actually composed of 6 state parks: Old Man's Cave, Cedar Falls, Ash Cave, Cantwell Cliffs, Rock House, and Conkle's Hollow. These areas, located along S.R. 374 and S.R. 56, encompass some of the most diverse and fascinating terrain in the state. The park and the surrounding buffer of state forest land shelter deeply cut gorges, cascading waterfalls, and mature forests. The Old Man's Cave region is the center of activity in the park as the campground, cabins, dining lodge, and park office are located there; a 17-acre lake is near the campground. There are hiking trails at each of the 6 parks, but a network of trails connect Ash Cave, Cedar Falls, and Old Man's Cave.

Facilities & Activities

170 camping sites
   129 sites with electricity
showers/flush toilets
dump station
laundry facilities
group camp (80 capacity)
youth group camp (160 capacity)
40 family housekeeping cabins
dining lodge (5/1-10/31)
   dining room and snack bar (accommodates 200)
   meeting room (accommodates 300)
   outdoor swimming pool (cabin guests + public)
picnicking, 4 picnic shelters
outdoor swimming pool at campground
summer nature programs
fishing, ice fishing
boating (electric motors only)
22 miles of hiking trails
portion of Buckeye Trail

Hueston Woods State Park

LEGEND

-))) Amphitheater
- ■ Change Booth
- ● Latrine
- ⋏ Picnic Area
- W Water
- Ⓛ Launch Ramps
- ⊞ Docks
- ▨ Nature Preserve

PICNIC AREAS

- A - Sycamore Grove
- B - Hedgerow
- C - Pine Grove
- D - Maple Grove
- E - Locust Grove
- F - Acton Lake
- G - Scenic Areas (No Picnicking)
- H - Quarry

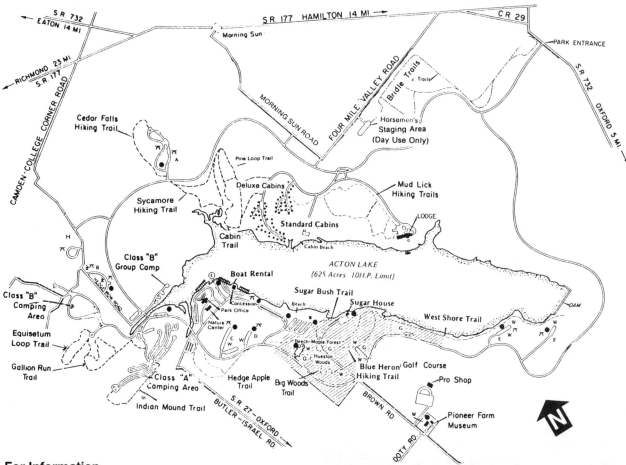

For Information

Hueston Woods State Park
Route 1
College Corner, OH 45003
(513) 523-1060 (camp office)
(513) 523-6381 (lodge)

Hueston Woods is one of 15 state parks in Ohio that offer cabins to rent; some are available year-round.

Hueston Woods State Park *(continued)*

Location

Hueston Woods State Park is located 5 miles north of Oxford. Recreational facilities at this 2,971-acre park surround Acton Lake and are accessible from U.S. 27, S.R. 732, and S.R. 177. The 625-acre lake, well-known for sailing, was formed by impounding water from Four Mile Creek; the lake lies in a northwest-southeast direction. The lodge and cabin complex are located on the northeast side of the lake. The lodge is a gigantic A-frame with a fabulous 100-foot high sandstone fireplace. Other facilities, including the park office, campground, 18-hole golf course, swimming beach, boat rental, and nature center, are located on the southwest side of the lake.

Eighteen-hole golf courses are located at five state parks: Deer Creek, Hueston Woods, Punderson, Salt Fork, and Shawnee.

Touching a snake isn't too scary as long as the park naturalist is willing to hold it.

Facilities & Activities

490 camping sites
   255 sites with electricity
showers/flush toilets
dump station
laundry facilities
4 group camps (100 capacity; 3 walk-in sites)
25 family housekeeping cabins
34 standard housekeeping cabins (4/1-10/31)
94-room resort lodge
   restaurant
   indoor/outdoor pools
   tennis
   18-hole golf course
pet camping area
picnicking
year-round Nature Center
summer nature programs
1,500-foot swimming beach
beach concession
fishing, ice fishing
boating (10-h.p. limit)
boat ramp/rental/seasonal dock rental
boat fuel/food service
cross-country skiing
sledding, ice skating, ice boating
15 miles of hiking trails
6 miles of bridle trails

Jackson Lake State Park

Legend
- 🅲 Picnic Shelter
- 🎏 Picnic Area
- 🅰 Camping
- ☐ Latrines
- 🅱 Fishing Access
- Ⓛ Launch Ramp
- ⛸ Ice Skating

For Information

Jackson Lake State Park
P.O. Box 174
921 Tommy Bean Road
Oak Hill, OH 45656
(614) 682-6197

Location

Jackson Lake State Park is located 2 miles west of Oakhill on S.R. 279. After crossing the causeway of the 242-acre lake, turn right to reach the park office and the campground. Rugged hills and mist-filled valleys provide a colorful backdrop for this 93-acre park; although relatively small, the park boasts some of the most scenic country in the state. Even in the heart of winter, when conditions are right, the park offers a well-maintained area for ice-skating just south of the causeway. Visitors to Jackson Lake should also take time to explore the Jefferson Iron Furnace, one of the last iron-smelting furnaces to shut down; the furnace is located just within the park boundaries.

Facilities & Activities

36 camping sites
pet camping area
picnicking, 3 picnic shelters
swimming beach
fishing
boating (10-h.p. limit)
3 boat ramps
sledding, ice skating

Although relatively small, this park boasts some of the most scenic country in the state.

John Bryan State Park

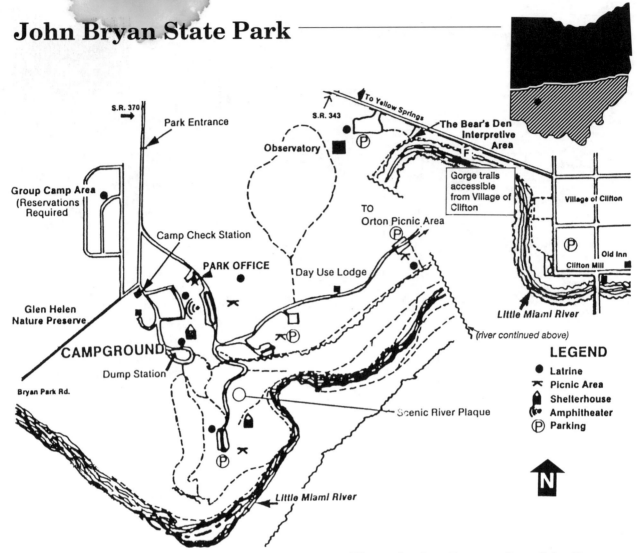

For Information

John Bryan State Park
3790 S.R. 370
Yellow Springs, OH 45387
(513) 767-1274

Location

John Bryan State Park is located on S.R. 370, just south of S.R. 343 that runs between Yellowspring and Clifton. The 750-acre park shelters a remarkable limestone gorge cut by the Little Miami River. A large section of this gorge is designated as the Clifton Gorge State Nature Preserve. The gorge has been designated as a National Natural Landmark by the U.S. Department of Interior. There are 10 different trails in the park; hikers should exercise caution when following the trails along the gorge. Some of the trails are also accessible from the village of Clifton.

The park takes its name from John Bryan, an ambitious businessman who was responsible for the preservation of much of the area as a state reserve. In 1896 Bryan purchased 335 acres along the gorge. Because he wanted to preserve the land for everyone to enjoy, he deeded it to the state when he drew up his will in 1916. In 1923, John Bryan's land became one of the state's first forest parks; in 1949 the park was placed in the hands of the newly-created Division of Parks and Recreation.

Facilities & Activities

100 camping sites
dump station
group camp (100 capacity)
picnicking, 2 picnic shelters
day-use lodge (rental)
summer nature programs
fishing
cross-country skiing, sledding
10 miles of hiking trails

Lake Alma State Park

For Information

Lake Alma State Park
P.O. Box 42
Wellston, OH 45692
(614) 384-4474

This park has 2 swimming beaches; both are picturesque and quite enticing.

Location

Lake Alma State Park is located 2 miles northeast of Wellston on S.R. 349; S.R. 349 is accessible from S.R. 93 on the north side of Wellston or from S.R. 160, west of Hamden. The 60-acre lake has a boat launch and 2 swimming beaches, as well as a 7-acre island accessible by foot bridge. Little Raccoon Creek, meandering through a wooded valley, provides a restful setting for the 219-acre park. The campground is located on the east side of the lake; several miles of hiking trails traverse hillcrests and valleys.

Facilities & Activities

60 camping sites with electricity
dump station
pet camping area
picnicking, 3 picnic shelters
2 swimming beaches
paved bicycle path
fishing
boating (electric motors only)
boat ramp
4 miles of hiking trails

Lake Hope State Park

For Information

Lake Hope State Park
Zaleski, OH 45698
(614) 596-5253

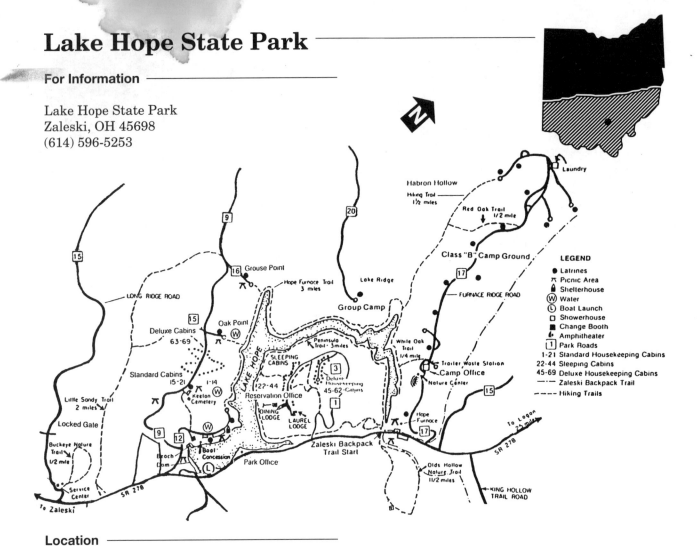

Location

Lake Hope State Park is located 4 miles northeast of Zaleski on S.R. 278. The 3,103-acre park and 120-acre lake are surrounded by the 2,500-acre Zaleski State Forest. There are 33 miles of bridle trails and 23½ miles of backpacking trails with campsites in the state forest; hunting is also allowed. The park is truly a nature lover's dream. Forest-draped hills invite exploration by hikers taking advantage of the park's trail system. The campground is located on Furnace Ridge Road; because of the rolling terrain, the campground is better suited for tent camping than for recreational vehicles. Overlooking shaded ravines, the cabin areas include all 3 types of cabins; 69 in all. The park office is just past the dam on the left, between the lake and S.R. 278.

Facilities & Activities

223 camping sites
  43 sites with electricity
showers
dump station
laundry facilities
5 rent-a-camp sites
youth group camp (100 capacity)
25 family housekeeping cabins
21 standard housekeeping cabins (4/1–10/31)
23 sleeping cabins (1–4 bedrooms)
rustic group lodge with kitchen (sleeps 24)
pet camping area
picnicking, picnic shelter
nature center
summer nature programs
600-foot swimming beach
beach concession
fishing, ice fishing
boating (electric motors only)
boat ramp/rental/food service
cross-country skiing
sledding, ice skating
13 miles of hiking trails
trailhead for the Zaleski State Forest backpack trail

Lake White State Park

For Information

Lake White State Park
2767 S.R. 551
Waverly, OH 45690
(614) 947-4059

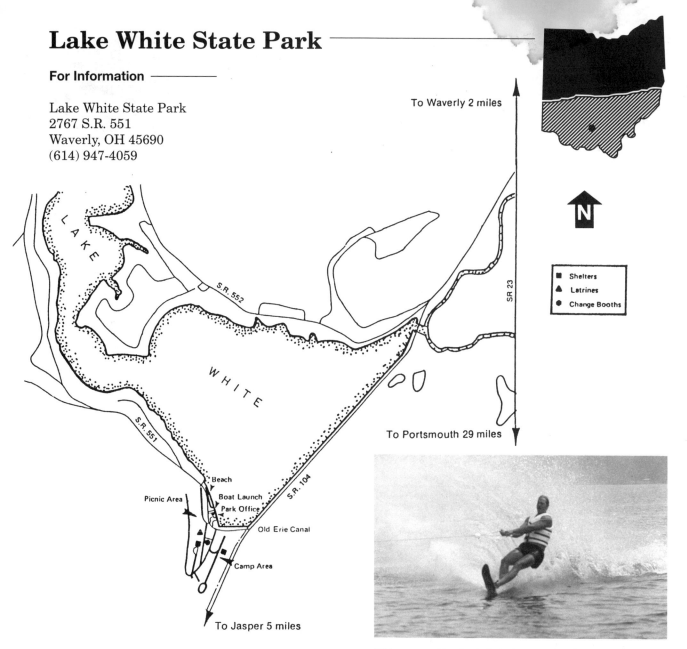

To Waverly 2 miles

N

■	Shelters
▲	Latrines
●	Change Booths

LAKE

WHITE

S.R. 552

S.R. 551

SR 23

To Portsmouth 29 miles

Beach
Picnic Area
Boat Launch
Park Office
S.R. 104
Old Erie Canal
Camp Area

To Jasper 5 miles

This waterskier is definitely not a beginner. Wow!

Location

Lake White State Park is located 4 miles south-west of Waverly, off S.R. 104. The 23-acre park is located near the southeast shore of the lake; most of the land surrounding the 337-acre lake is privately owned. The lake lies between 2 ridges of rugged hills, near the flood plain of the Scioto River. A well-known event in the region is the fourth of July boat parade held annually at the park. Part of the park includes the remains of the abandoned Ohio and Erie Canal; the small campground, separated from the lake by S.R. 551, is tucked in the bed of the old canal channel.

Facilities & Activities

38 camping sites
dump station
boat dock/tie-ups at campground
picnicking, 2 picnic shelters
50-foot swimming beach
fishing
boating/water skiing
boat ramp
sledding, ice skating

Muskingum River Parkway

The parkway office is at Lock 10 in Zanesville; it is accessible by boat or by foot from the Canal Bridge off 6th Street. Information on the river and the parkway can be obtained from the office or at any of the locks. If planning a trip on the Muskingum River Parkway, be sure to obtain navigational charts and the latest bulletin on hours of operation for the locks. A small primitive campground is located at Ellis off of S.R. 60 and C.R. 49. This Lock #11 campground has water, picnic tables, fire rings, latrines, public phone, and a launching ramp. Several of the campsites are located along the Muskingum River.

LEGEND

x	PICNICKING
●	LATRINE
W	DRINKING WATER
L	BOAT LAUNCH

For Information

Muskingum River Parkway
P.O. Box 2806
Hughes & 8th Street
Zanesville, OH 43702
(614) 452-3820

Location

The Muskingum River parallels S.R. 60 for most of the distance between Dresden (north of Zanesville) and Marietta (on the Ohio River). The original navigable waterway was completed in 1841. The Division of Parks and Recreation now operates the 10 locks, numbered from 2 through 11, encompassing 120 acres of land and controlling 93 miles of scenic waterway from Marietta to Dresden. The river channel from Dresden to Ellis is unmarked and hard to follow. Dresden, on the west bank above Ellis is where the Ohio Canal was connected by locks to the Muskingum. Some of the tributaries that empty into the Muskingum River are also navigable for short distances.

Facilities & Activities

20 camping sites (at Lock #11)
pet camping area
picnicking (at all locks except #9)
fishing
boating (houseboats, pontoon boats, canoe & rowboats)
boat ramps (at Locks #4, 5, 6 & 11)
1 mile of hiking trails

Paint Creek State Park

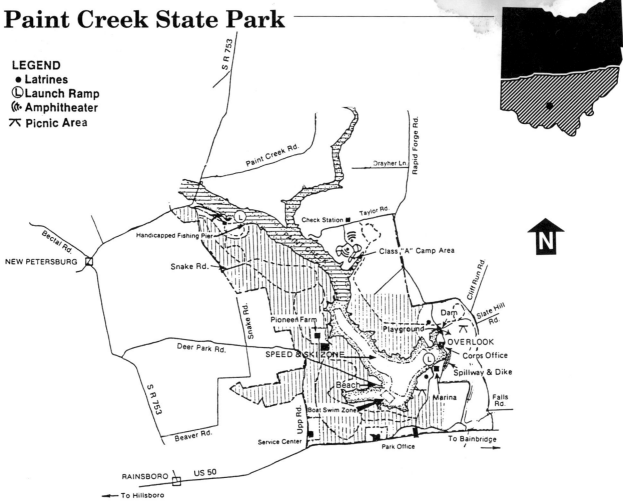

LEGEND
- ● Latrines
- Ⓛ Launch Ramp
- ⟨ⱡ⟩ Amphitheater
- ⟅ Picnic Area

For Information

Paint Creek State Park
14265 U.S. 50
Bainbridge, OH 45612
(513) 365-1401
(513) 981-7061 (camp office)

Location

Paint Creek State Park is located 17 miles east of Hillsboro off of U.S. 50. The region lies at the very edge of the Appalachian Plateau. This escarpment marks the boundary between the hilly eastern section of the state and the flatter western portions. The 9,000-acre park boasts one of the newest campgrounds in the state; it is on the east shore overlooking the 1,200-acre lake and is reached by traveling north on Rapid Forge Road. On the west side of the lake is Paint Creek Pioneer Farm. The working farm includes a log house, a collection of log buildings, livestock, gardens, and croplands. The buildings are furnished to create an atmosphere of the early 1800s, the settlement period of south-

western Ohio. Travel north on Upp Road to reach the farm; the park office is on U.S. 50 just past Upp Road.

Facilities & Activities

199 camping sites with electricity
showers/flush toilets
dump station
3 rent-a-camp sites
pet camping area
picnicking
1,000-foot swimming beach
hunting, fishing
boating/water skiing
3 boat ramps
boat rental/seasonal dock rental
boat fuel
snowmobiling
cross-country skiing, sledding
ice skating
8 miles of hiking trails
25 miles of bridle trails

Pike Lake State Park

BAINBRIDGE 6 miles

T-348

DELUXE CABINS
#19 - #26

DELUXE CABIN
#15

CONCESSION
BATH HOUSE
BEACH

BUCKEYE TRAIL

STANDARD CABINS
#3 - #14

GROUP LODGE

Pike Lake

DELUXE CABINS
#16 - 18
STANDARD CABIN #2
PARK OFFICE

BOAT RENTAL
CONCESSION

DAM

NATURE CENTER
T-505

WILDLIFE
DISPLAY

GROUP
CAMP AREA
HORSESHOE COURT
BASKETBALL COURT

DUMP STATION
SOFTBALL FIELD
CAMP OFFICE

PLAYGROUND

CLASS "B" CAMP AREA

NON-ELECTRIC SITES

T-348

LEGEND
- Latrine
- Water Fountain
- Picnic Area
- Amphitheater
- Trail

Facilities & Activities

112 camping sites
  101 sites with electricity
dump station
camp commissary
group camp (30 capacity)
12 family housekeeping cabins
13 standard housekeeping cabins (4/1–10/31)
picnicking
nature center, summer nature programs
155-foot swimming beach
beach concession
fishing, ice fishing
boating (electric motors only)
sledding, ice skating
3½ miles of hiking trails
3-mile portion of Buckeye Trail

For Information

Pike Lake State Park
1847 Pike Lake Road
Bainbridge, OH 45612
(614) 493-2212

Location

Pike Lake State Park is located southwest of Chillicothe, accessible from U.S. 50 near Bainbridge from the north, or from S.R. 124 off of S.R. 32 from the south. The 600-acre park is 5 miles northwest of Morgantown on Pike Lake Road (T-348). Situated in wooded hill country, the park is a hiker's paradise. There are also 10 miles of bridle trails in the nearby 11,621-acre Pike State Forest for horseback riding enthusiasts. The cabins are situated on a hillside with a scenic view of the lake valley and surrounding hills. A beautiful swimming area is located at the 13-acre lake.

A beautiful swimming area is located at the 13-acre Pike Lake; a beach concession is nearby.

Rocky Fork State Park

For Information

Rocky Fork State Park
9800 N. Shore Drive
Hillsboro, OH 45133
(513) 393-4284

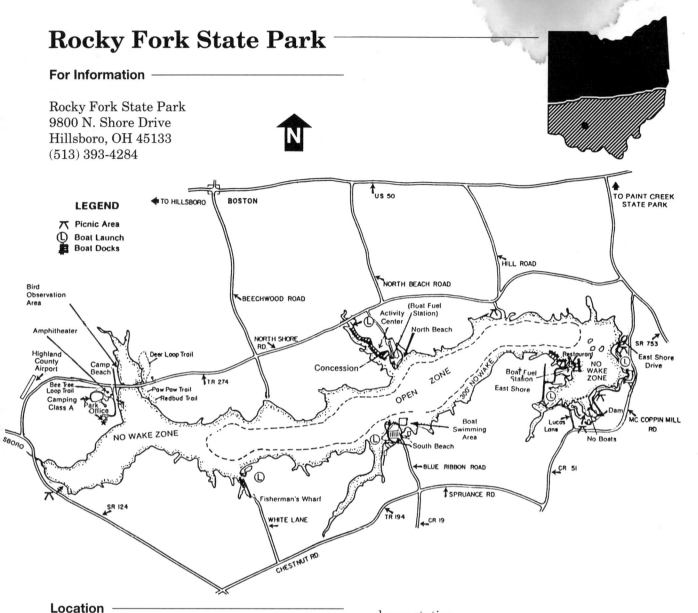

LEGEND
- 🛆 Picnic Area
- Ⓛ Boat Launch
- 🚢 Boat Docks

Location

Rocky Fork State Park is located 6 miles south-east of Hillsboro. The park office, campground, and a marina are located at the west end of the lake on North Shore Road off of S.R. 124. The 2 swimming beaches, restaurant, boat launches, and 2 other marinas are at various locations around the lake, accessible from U.S. 50, S.R. 753, or S.R. 506. The 1,384-acre park is a recreational getaway for the active outdoorsperson. The 2,080-acre lake has become a favorite of anglers and water sports enthusiasts.

Facilities & Activities

220 camping sites
  70 sites with electricity
showers/flush toilets
dump station
laundry facilities
camp commissary
beach at campground
boat dock/tie-ups at campground
boat launch at campground
pet camping area
picnicking, picnic shelters
East Shore Marina Restaurant (5/1–10/31)
summer nature programs
2 swimming beaches
beach concession
hunting, fishing, ice fishing
boating/water skiing
5 boat ramps
boat rental/seasonal dock rental
boat fuel/food service
sledding
4 miles of hiking trails

Scioto Trail State Park

For Information

Scioto Trail State Park
144 Lake Road
Chillicothe, OH 45601
(614) 663-2125

LEGEND
- Roads
- Trail
- Stream
- Picnic Area
- Toilets

N

Location

Scioto Trail State Park is located south of Chillicothe and east of U.S. 23/S.R. 104 on S.R. 372. The 218-acre park is nestled in beautiful Scioto Trail State Forest; the ridgetops and winding forest roads offer breathtaking vistas. The park office, campground, and the historical log church are located near Caldwell Lake, one of the two small lakes at the park. The church is a replica of the first church in the area when white settlers came in the 1770s. Scioto Trail received its name for one of the wagon trails traveled by settlers from Portsmouth to the first capital of Ohio, Chillicothe. When snow conditions allow, Scioto Trail opens its sledding hill, perhaps the largest designated sledding hill in the state. There are 17 miles of bridle trails on the surrounding 9,371 acres of state forest lands.

Facilities & Activities

58 camping sites
   20 sites with electricity
dump station
boat launch at campground
group camp (100 capacity; walk-in sites; tents only)
12 primitive walk-in campsites
pet camping area
picnicking
hunting, fishing, ice fishing
boating (electric motors only)
boat ramp
cross-country skiing
sledding, ice skating
12 miles of hiking trails
portion of Buckeye Trail

Seneca Lake

For Information

Seneca Lake Park
22172 Park Road
Senecaville, OH 43780
(614) 685-6013 (Lake Park)
(614) 685-5831 (Seneca marina)

*Coming in under power
after a great day of
sailing.*

Location

Seneca Lake is east of Buffalo, via S.R. 313; from I-77, take exit 37 and head east. The 3,550-acre lake has a 4,063-acre land area. The lake has 2 campgrounds; Marina Point, adjacent to the full-service marina, and Seneca Lake Park. Marina Point is northeast of the dam off of S.R. 313; Seneca Lake Park is southeast of the dam. The park entrance is on S.R. 574, off of S.R. 313 at the dam. Seneca Point is open April 1–October 31; Seneca Lake Park is open year-round. Pets are permitted in designated areas.

Facilities & Activities

Marina Point—320 campsites
  electric hookups
  flush toilets/hot showers
Lake Park—250 campsites
  hookups (all electric; 78 full)
  flush toilets/hot showers

vacation cabins (sleep 6)
camper cabins
picnic areas/grills
group shelter
playground
miniature golf course
swimming beach
concession stand
nature center
amphitheater
hiking trails
hunting
Marina (& lake activities)
  fishing
  boating/waterskiing (180 h.p. maximum)
  bait/tackle/supplies
  lunch counter
  boat ramp/docks/boat rentals
portion of Buckeye Trail

Shawnee State Park

This park, nestled in the Shawnee State Forest, provides a multitude of trails, including cross-country ski trails.

Legend
- ⊄ – Amphitheater
- ▲ – Shelter House
- ● – Latrine
- ✗ – Picnic Area
- ■ – Change Booth
- □ – Washhouse

For Information

Shawnee State Park
Star Route 125, P.O. Box 68
Portsmouth, OH 45662
(614) 858-4561 (camp office)
(614) 858-6621 (lodge/cabins)

Location

Shawnee State Park is located west of Portsmouth off of S.R. 125; from Portsmouth, travel southwest on U.S. 52 along the Ohio River, then northwest on S.R. 125. Located in the Appalachian foothills bordering the Ohio River, the park is nestled in the 59,603-acre Shawnee State Forest. The Shawnee area is known as the "Little Smokies of Ohio." The state forest boasts a multitude of trails including a popular 50-mile backpack trail and miles of bridle trails. An equestrian campground is also located in the state forest.

This 1,100-acre park is a multi-million dollar recreational area and includes one of the state's 7 resort lodges. The campground is bordered on one side by one of the park's 2 small lakes (68 acres total), and by a cascading stream on the other. The golf course is located on U.S. 52, adjacent to the park's marina that provides access to the Ohio River.

Facilities & Activities

107 camping sites
   104 sites with electricity
showers/flush toilets
dump station
25 family housekeeping cabins
50-room resort lodge
   restaurant
   indoor/outdoor pools
   tennis
   18-hole golf course
pet camping area
picnicking, 2 picnic shelters
nature center, summer nature programs
swimming beach
beach concession
hunting, fishing, ice fishing
boating (electric motors only)
3 boat ramps
boat rental/seasonal dock rental
boat fuel/food service
cross-country skiing, ice skating
5 miles of hiking trails

Stonelick State Park

Stonelick State Park
Route 1, Box 343
Pleasant Plain, OH 45162
(513) 625-7544
(513) 625-6593 (camp office)

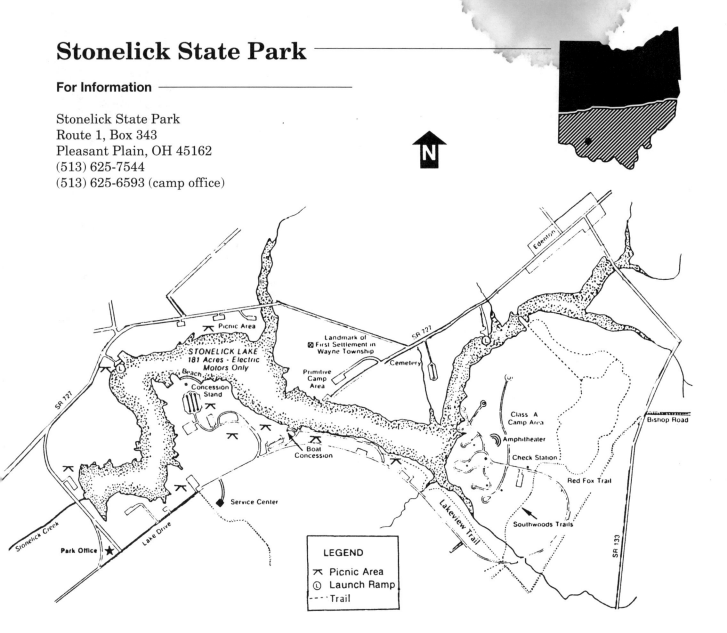

Location

Stonelick State Park is located at Edenton along S.R. 727 and S.R. 133. This 1,058-acre park is rather special in that it was established to provide a recreation area for Ohio's water sports enthusiasts. Boating, fishing, and swimming are popular at the 200-acre lake. The campground has both sunny and shaded sites. Numerous picnic areas are located around the lake. The park office is located at the southwest corner of the park off of S.R. 727.

Facilities & Activities

153 camping sites
showers/flush toilets
dump station
laundry facilities
5 rent-a-camp sites
group camp (150 capacity; walk-in sites)
pet camping area
picnicking
summer nature programs
swimming beach
hunting, fishing
boating (electric motors only)
2 boat ramps
cross-country skiing
sledding
ice skating
7 miles of hiking trails

Strouds Run State Park

For Information

Strouds Run State Park
11661 State Park Road
Athens, OH 45701
(614) 592-2302

Large blocks of uninterrupted hardwood forest surround Dow Lake; a hiking trail passes through as it encircles the lake.

Location

Strouds Run State Park is located 5 miles east of Athens on C.R. 20, which runs east and west between Athens and S.R. 690. The 2,606-acre park contains some of the largest blocks of uninterrupted hardwood forest in the county. The park derives its name from a family named Strouds, who settled in the area in the 1800s. The dam creating the 161-acre Dow Lake is not the only dam on Strouds Run; a colony of beaver has constructed dams of its own north of the lake. The campground is located along Strouds Run; the park office is about 1 mile north on Township Road 212.

Facilities & Activities

80 camping sites
dump station
4 rent-a-camp sites
youth group camp (40 capacity; tents only)

pet camping area
picnicking, picnic shelter
900-foot swimming beach
beach concession
scuba diving
hunting, fishing, ice fishing
fishing pier
boating (10-h.p. limit)
boat ramp/rental/boat docks
sledding, ice skating
13 miles of hiking trails

Tar Hollow State Park

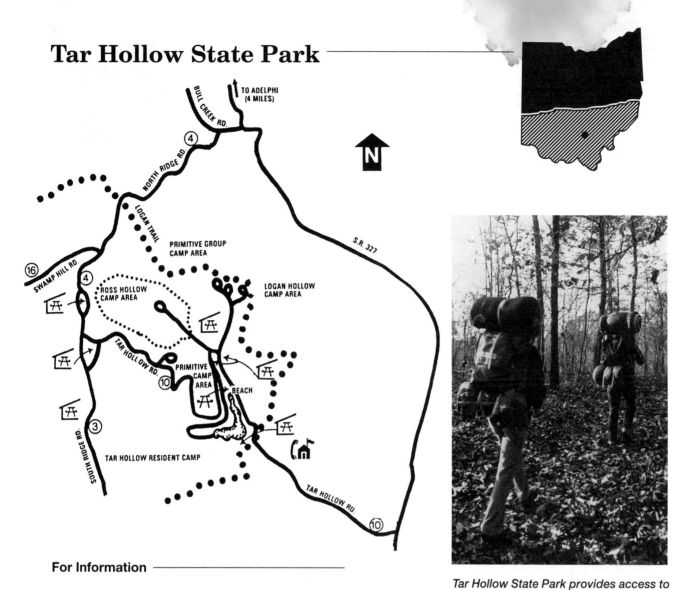

Tar Hollow State Park provides access to the 21-mile Logan backpacking trail.

For Information

Tar Hollow State Park
16396 Tar Hollow Road
Laurelville, OH 43135
(614) 887-4818

Location

Tar Hollow State Park is located 10 miles south of Adelphi off S.R. 327 and is surrounded by the rugged foothills of the Appalachian plateau. The region derives its name from pine tar, an essential commodity in early Ohio households; it was taken from the knots and heartwood of the native pitch pine tree. The 619-acre park is surrounded by the 16,126-acre Tar Hollow State Forest. Nine miles of bridle trails and the 21-mile Logan backpacking trail are located on the state forest lands. The steep-banked 15-acre Pine Lake has restricted shoreline fishing but offers excellent opportunities to fishermen with canoes or other light boats that are relatively easy to launch.

Facilities & Activities

96 camping sites
showers
dump station
group camp (100 capacity)
16 primitive walk-in campsites
resident camp (5/1–10/31)
pet camping area
picnicking, picnic shelters
swimming beach
hunting, fishing
boating (electric motors only)
boat ramp
4 miles of hiking trails
trailhead of Logan Trail
portion of Buckeye Trail

Wayne National Forest

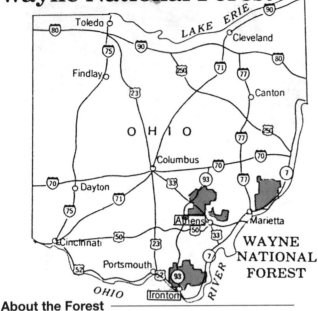

For Information

Forest Supervisor
Wayne-Hoosier
National Forest
811 Constitution Avenue
Bedford, IN 47421
(812) 275-5987

About the Forest

The Wayne National Forest is located in southeastern Ohio and covers approximately 200,000 acres in the foothills of the Appalachian Mountains. Rugged hills covered with diverse stands of hardwoods, pine, and cedar; lakes, river, and streams; springs, rock-shelters, and covered bridges, all characterize the Wayne National Forest. The Wayne is made up of three units, separated geographically—the Ironton, the Athens, and the Marietta. For supervisory purposes, there are two ranger districts, the Ironton and the Athens, with the latter including the Marietta Unit. For administration, the Wayne is linked with the Hoosier National Forest in Indiana.

Materials on recreational opportunities in the Wayne National Forest are available from each of the three offices as well as from the office of the forest supervisor. All national forest lands are available for primitive camping, hiking, fishing and hunting; contact them for maps and specific information. They also have information on such items as winter activities; river trips for canoeists; hiking, backpacking, and horse trails; and opening and closing dates for campgrounds.

Facilities on the Wayne National Forest include 3 campgrounds, with 86 units, 2 group camps, 46 miles of horse trails, 100 miles of hiking trails, 69 miles of ORV trails, swimming beach, picnic areas, boat ramps and 4 canoe access points on the Little Muskingum River. The 18-mile Stone Church Horse Trail, the 15-mile Wildcat Hollow Backpacking Trail, and a portion of the North Country/Buckeye Trail are all on the Athens Ranger District. Camp-

ing may be done in small openings along the backpacking trails; *do not* cut understory vegetation to create a campsite.

The Little Muskingum River, that flows placidly through some of the most beautiful scenery in Ohio, is on the Marietta Unit of the Athens Ranger District. The upper part of the river above the Clear Fork junction (3 miles south of Ring Mill) can best be enjoyed in early spring when water levels are highest. Below Clear Fork the river is large enough to permit canoeing most of the year. This provides some 33 miles of easy paddling. At normal water levels, the river presents no significant difficulties or hazards, even to the novice. The canoe access points to the Little Muskingum River are northeast of Marietta along S.R. 26. They are Ring Mill, Haught Run, Hune Bridge and Lane Farm. Each of these canoe access points have several campsites.

The Marietta Unit, known for its many covered bridges, has several developed picnic areas as well as miles of hiking/backpacking trails. The Marietta portion of the North Country Trail is now 35 miles long; including side trails, it totals 53 miles. Other trails include the 3.4-mile Scenic River Trail, the 7-mile Ohio View Trail and 5 miles of the Lamping Homestead Trails. For information on the hiking trails and canoeing the Little Muskingum River, contact the Marietta Unit at:

Marietta Unit
RR #1, Box 132
Marietta, OH 45750
(614) 373-9055

Athens Ranger District

For Information

Athens Ranger District
219 Columbus Road
Athens, OH 45701
(614) 592-6644

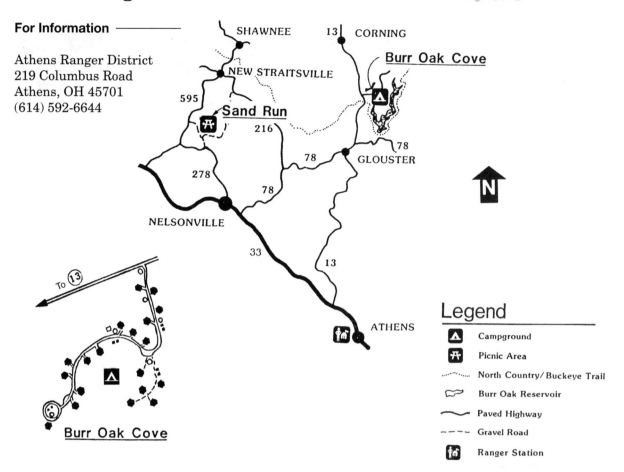

Legend

▲	Campground
☕	Picnic Area
⋯⋯	North Country/Buckeye Trail
⌒	Burr Oak Reservoir
—	Paved Highway
- - -	Gravel Road
👥	Ranger Station

Campground Location

Burr Oak Cove Campground is the only national forest campground in the Athens Ranger District. The primitive campground is ½ mile east of S.R. 13, which runs between Corning and Glouster. It is adjacent to Burr Oak State Park in a densely wooded area on the northwest tip of Burr Oak Reservoir; the 1-mile Lake View Trail provides easy access to the scenic lake. The campground is open May 15 through the close of deer season on December 7.

Facilities & Activities

19 campsites
   (5 are walk-in sites)
tables
fire rings
pit toilets
drinking water
hiking
portion of Buckeye Trail

This bulletin board at Burr Oak Cove Campground is typical for self-registration campgrounds found in many national and state forests.

**OHIO
REGION 2**

Athens Ranger District   155

Ironton Ranger District

For Information

Ironton Ranger District
710 Park Avenue
Ironton, OH 45638
(614) 532-3223

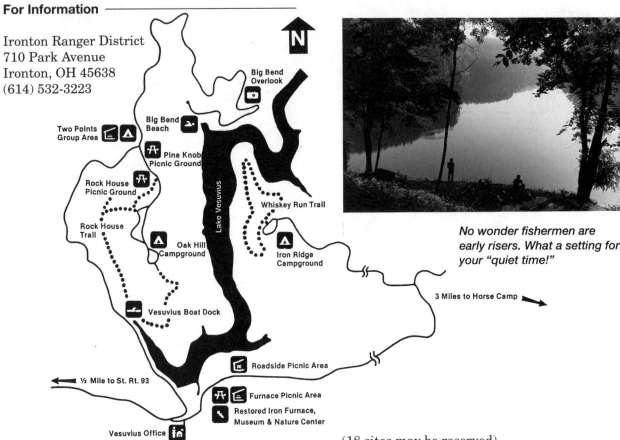

No wonder fishermen are early risers. What a setting for your "quiet time!"

Campground Locations

Lake Vesuvius Recreation Area is located ½-mile off of S.R. 93, about 10 miles northeast of Ironton; Ironton, on U.S. 52, borders the Ohio River. The area gets its name from the old iron blast furnace that stands near the dam. The Vesuvius furnace was one of the first iron blast furnaces in the famous Hanging Rock Iron District. It was built in 1833 and continued in operation until 1906.

The recreation area has 2 family campgrounds, a group camping area, and a horse camp. **Oak Hill Campground** and the group camping area at Two Points are located on the west side of the lake; **Iron Ridge Campground** and the horse camp are on the east side. The equestrian camp is the trailhead for the 28-mile loop trail. Facilities throughout the Vesuvius Recreation Area are handicapped accessible. For camping reservations call 1-800-283-CAMP.

Facilities and Activities

Oak Hill Campground
    24 campsites with electric hookups
    (18 sites may be reserved)
    flush toilets/hot showers
    open: 4/20–10/31
Iron Ridge Campground
    20 drive-in campsites
    23 walk-in, tents-only campsites
    (all available for reservation)
    pit-type toilets
    open year-round
Two Points Group Camp
    primitive
    2 sites (each accommodates 100)
    (by reservation only)
Horse Camp
    primitive; no running water
    hitching rails
picnicking, picnic shelters (reservations)
nature center/museum
swimming beach (fee)
fishing
boating (no motors)
boat/canoe rentals
boat launch/dock
over 9 miles of hiking trails
16-mile backpack trail
28-mile horse trail

West Fork of Mill Creek Lake

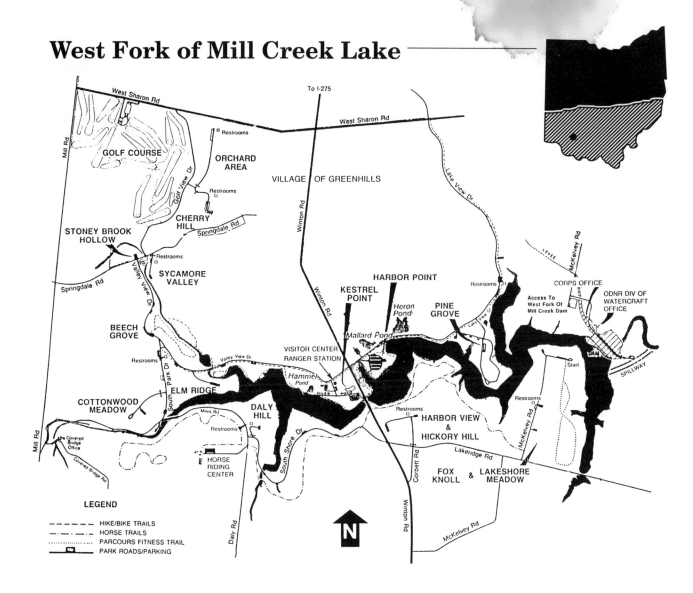

For Information

Hamilton County Park District
10245 Winton Road
Cincinnati, OH 45231
(513) 521-7275
(513) 851-2267 (campground)

Location

West Fork of Mill Creek Lake is also known to many as Winton Woods Park. Through a cooperative agreement with the U.S. Army Corps of Engineers, Hamilton County Park District operates the recreational facilities and activities at the park. The 183-acre lake (normal pool) is situated on the West Fork of Mill Creek about 10 miles north of Cincinnati and south of I-275. The dam is 18 miles above the entrance of Mill Creek into the Ohio River. Access to the lake area is provided by Win-

ton Road, Hamilton Avenue (U.S. 127), and numerous improved county roads. The ranger station and visitor center is north of the lake on Valley View Drive, just west of Winton Road. The campground is on the north side of the lake at Pine Grove; go east on Lake View Drive from Winton Road.

Facilities & Activities

80 campsites
  40 with electricity
flush toilets/hot showers
picnic areas
golf course
riding stables
playgrounds/play fields
3-mile hike/bike trail
fishing
rowboat/paddleboat rentals

Wolf Run State Park

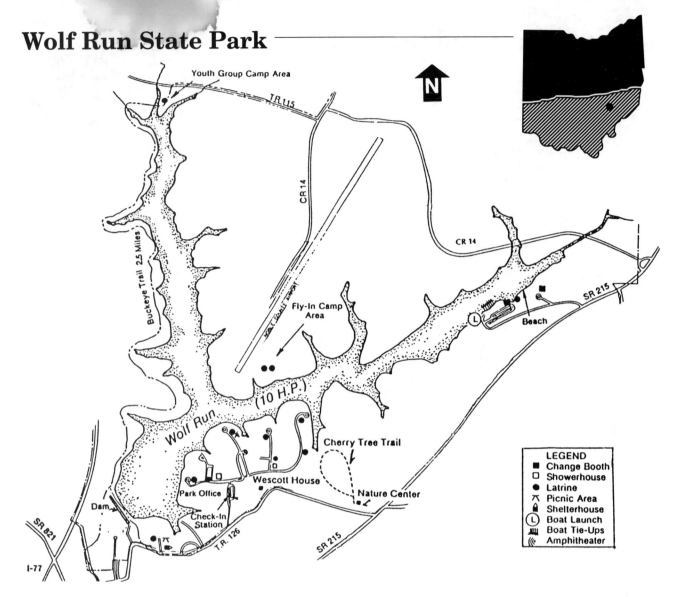

For Information

Wolf Run State Park
16170 Wolf Run Road
Caldwell, OH 43724
(614) 732-5035

Location

Wolf Run State Park is located ½-mile east of the
Belle Valley exit 28 on I-77. At the junction of S.R.
821, take S.R. 215. The entrance to the office and
camping area is on Bond Ridge Road off S.R. 215;
the swimming beach and boat launch area entrance
is also off S.R. 215. The rolling hills of southeast
Ohio provide the setting for this 1,143-acre park;
it received its name from the first family, the Wolfs,
that moved into the valley. Scuba diving is permitted in the 220-acre lake, except in the beach
area; diving alone is not permitted.

Facilities & Activities

140 camping sites
showers
dump station
laundry facilities
youth group camp (120 capacity; tents only)
20-site primitive fly-in camping area
pet camping area
picnicking, picnic shelter
swimming beach
scuba diving
hunting, fishing, ice fishing
boating (10-h.p. limit)
launch ramp
boat tie-ups
cross-country skiing
sledding, ice skating
2½-mile portion of Buckeye Trail

Camping/Backpacking Supplies Checklists

Camping Equipment Checklist

The following checklists are designed to guide you in planning your next camping trip. Your needs will vary according to the type, length, and destination of your trip, as well as personal preferences, number of persons included, season of the year, and budget limitations.

Obviously, all items on the checklists aren't needed on any one trip. Since using checklists helps you think more methodically in planning, these extensive lists should serve merely as a reminder of items you may need.

When using these checklists to plan a trip, the item may be checked (√) if it needs to be taken. Upon returning, if the item was considered unnecessary, a slash could be used: ⅄. If a needed item was forgotten, a zero could be used (0); if the item has been depleted and needs to be replenished, an encircling of the check could be used; Ⓥ. This is of particular importance if you camp regularly and keep a camping box packed with staples that can be ready to go on a moment's notice.

Cooking equipment needs are quite dependent on the menu—whether you plan to cook and eat three balanced meals a day or whether you plan to eat non-cooked meals or snacks the entire trip. Many campers find it helpful to jot down the proposed menu for each meal on a 4″ × 6″ index card to help determine the grocery list as well as the equipment needed to prepare the meal. By planning this way, you'll avoid taking equipment you'll never use and you won't forget important items.

Typical Menu with Grocery and Equipment Needs

MEAL: Saturday breakfast		Number of Persons: 5
MENU	GROCERY LIST	EQUIPMENT
orange juice	Tang	camp stove
bacon	10 slices bacon	gasoline, funnel
eggs	8 eggs	folding oven
(scrambled)	1 can biscuits	frying pan
biscuits	peach jelly	baking pan
	honey	pitcher
	margarine	mixing bowl
	salt	cooking fork, spoon
	pepper	

Shelter/Sleeping:

_____ Air mattresses
_____ Air mattress pump
_____ Cots, folding
_____ Cot pads
_____ Ground cloth
_____ Hammock
_____ Mosquito netting
_____ Sleeping bag or bed roll
_____ Tarps (plastic & canvas)
_____ Tent
_____ Tent stakes, poles, guy ropes
_____ Tent repair kit
_____ Whisk broom

Extra Comfort:

_____ Camp stool
_____ Catalytic heater
_____ Folding chairs

_____ Folding table
_____ Fuel for lantern & heater
_____ Funnel
_____ Lantern
_____ Mantels for lantern
_____ Toilet, portable
_____ Toilet chemicals
_____ Toilet bags
_____ Wash basin

Clothing/Personal Gear:

_____ Bathing suit
_____ Boots, hiking & rain
_____ Cap/hat
_____ Facial tissues
_____ Flashlight (small), batteries
_____ Jacket/windbreaker
_____ Jeans/trousers
_____ Pajamas

_____ Pocket knife
_____ Poncho
_____ Prescription drugs
_____ Rain suit
_____ Sheath knife
_____ Shirts
_____ Shoes
_____ Shorts
_____ Socks
_____ Sweat shirt/sweater
_____ Thongs (for showering)
_____ Toilet articles (comb, soap, shaving equipment, tooth brush, toothpaste, mirror, etc.)
_____ Toilet paper
_____ Towels
_____ Underwear
_____ Washcloth

Safety/Health:

_____ First-aid kit
_____ First-aid manual
_____ Fire extinguisher
_____ Insect bite remedy
_____ Insect repellant
_____ Insect spray/bomb
_____ Poison ivy lotion
_____ Safety pins
_____ Sewing repair kit
_____ Scissors
_____ Snake bite kit
_____ Sunburn lotion
_____ Suntan cream
_____ Water purifier

Optional:

_____ Binoculars
_____ Camera, film, tripod,
       light meter
_____ Canteen
_____ Compass
_____ Fishing tackle
_____ Frisbee, horseshoes,
       washers, etc.
_____ Games for car travel &
       rainy day
_____ Hobby equipment
_____ Identification books:
       birds, flowers, rocks,
       stars, trees, etc.
_____ Knapsack/day pack for
       hikes
_____ Magnifying glass
_____ Map of area
_____ Notebook & pencil
_____ Sunglasses

Miscellaneous:

_____ Bucket/pail
_____ Candles
_____ Clothesline
_____ Clothespins
_____ Electrical extension cord
_____ Flashlight (large),
       batteries
_____ Hammer
_____ Hand axe/hatchet
_____ Nails
_____ Newspapers
_____ Pliers
_____ Rope
_____ Saw, bow or folding
_____ Sharpening stone/file
_____ Shovel
_____ Tape, masking or plastic
_____ Twine/cord
_____ Wire
_____ Work gloves

Cooking Equipment Checklist

Food Preparation/ Serving/Storing:

_____ Aluminum foil
_____ Bags (large & small,
       plastic & paper)
_____ Bottle/juice can opener
_____ Bowls, nested with lids
       for mixing, serving &
       storing
_____ Can opener
_____ Colander
_____ Fork, long-handled
_____ Ice chest
_____ Ice pick
_____ Knife, large
_____ Knife, paring
_____ Ladle for soups & stews
_____ Measuring cup
_____ Measuring spoon
_____ Pancake turner
_____ Potato & carrot peeler
_____ Recipes
_____ Rotary beater
_____ Spatula
_____ Spoon, large
_____ Tongs
_____ Towels, paper
_____ Water jug
_____ Wax paper/plastic wrap

Cooking:

_____ Baking pans
_____ Charcoal
_____ Charcoal grill (hibachi or
       small collapsible type)
_____ Charcoal lighter
_____ Coffee pot
_____ Cook kit, nested/pots &
       pans with lids
_____ Fuel for stove
       (gasoline/kerosene/liquid
       propane)
_____ Griddle
_____ Hot pads/asbestos gloves
_____ Matches
       Ovens for baking:
_____ Cast iron dutch oven
_____ Folding oven for fuel
       stoves
_____ Reflector oven
_____ Tote oven
_____ Skewers
_____ Skillet with cover
_____ Stove, portable
_____ Toaster (folding camp
       type)
_____ Wire grill for open fire

Eating:

_____ Bowls for cereal, salad,
       soup
_____ Cups, paper
_____ Forks
_____ Glasses, plastic
_____ Knives
_____ Napkins, paper
_____ Pitcher, plastic
_____ Plates (plastic, alu-
       minum, paper)
_____ Spoons
_____ Table cloth, plastic
_____
_____

Clean-Up:

_____ Detergent (Bio-degrad-
       able soap)
_____ Dish pan
_____ Dish rag
_____ Dish towels
_____ Scouring pad
_____ Scouring powder
_____ Sponge

Hiking/Backpacking Checklist

This list is not meant to be all inclusive or necessary for each trip. It is a guide in choosing the proper gear. Although this list was prepared for the hiker/backpacker, it is quite appropriate for anyone using the backcountry, whether they are traveling by foot, canoe, bicycle, or horse. Parentheses indicate those optional items that you may not want to carry depending upon the length of the trip, weather conditions, personal preferences, or necessity.

Ten Essentials for Any Trip:

___ Map
___ Compass
___ First-aid kit
___ Pocket knife
___ Signaling device
___ Extra clothing
___ Extra food
___ Small flashlight/extra bulb & batteries
___ Fire starter/candle/waterproof matches
___ Sunglasses

Day Trip (add to the above):

___ Comfortable boots or walking shoes
___ Rain parka or 60/40 parka
___ Day Pack
___ Water bottle/canteen bottle/canteen
___ Cup
___ Water purification tablets
___ Insect repellant
___ Sun lotion
___ Chapstick
___ Food
___ Brimmed hat
___ (Guide book)
___ Toilet paper & trowel
___ (Camera & film)
___ (Binoculars)
___ (Book)
___ Wallet & I.D.
___ Car key & coins for phone
___ Moleskin for blisters
___ Whistle

Overnight or Longer Trips (add the following):

___ Backpack
___ Sleeping bag
___ Foam pad
___ (Tent)
___ (Bivouac cover)
___ (Ground cloth/poncho)
___ Stove
___ Extra fuel
___ Cooking pot(s)
___ Pot scrubber
___ Spoon (knife & fork)
___ (Extra cup/bowl)
___ Extra socks
___ Extra shirt(s)
___ Extra pants/shorts
___ Extra underwear
___ Wool shirt/sweater
___ (Camp shoes)
___ Bandana
___ (Gloves)
___ (Extra water container)
___ Nylon cord
___ Extra matches
___ Soap
___ Toothbrush/powder/floss
___ Mirror
___ Medicines
___ (Snake bite kit)
___ (Notebook & pencil)
___ Licenses & permits
___ (Playing cards)
___ (Zip-lock bags)
___ (Rip stop repair tape)
___ Repair kit—wire, rivets, pins, buttons, thread, needle, boot strings

Indiana Resources

Indiana Department of Commerce
Division of Tourism
One North Capitol, Suite 700
Indianapolis, IN 46204
1-800-289-6646 (to request printed material)
1-800-782-3775 (for other tourism information)

Indiana Department of Natural Resources
402 W. Washington St.
Indianapolis, IN 46204

   Division of Fish and Wildlife
   Room 273
   (317) 232-4080

   Division of Forestry
   Room 296
   (317) 232-4105

Division of Outdoor Recreation
Room 271
(317) 232-4070

Division of Public Information and Education
Room 264
(317) 232-4200

Division of Reservoir Management
Room 282
(317) 232-4060

Division of State Parks
Room 298
(317) 232-4124
1-800-622-4931 (Indiana residents outside
   Indianapolis)

Ohio Resources

Ohio Department of Development
Division of Travel and Tourism
(30 E. Broad Street, 23rd Floor)
P.O. Box 1001
Columbus, OH 43266-0101
1-800-BUCKEYE (nationwide)

Ohio Department of Natural Resources
Fountain Square
1952 Belcher Drive
Columbus, OH 43224

   Division of Forestry
   Building C-3
   (614) 265-6694

Division of Parks and Recreation
Building C-1
(614) 265-7000

Division of Natural Areas & Preserves
Building F-1
(614) 265-6453

Division of Watercraft
Building C-2
(614) 265-6480

Publications Center
Building B-1
(614) 265-6608

Other Resources

Buckeye Trail Association
P.O. Box 254
Worthington, OH 43085
(513) 275-8972

Cuyahoga Valley National Recreation Area
15610 Vaughn Road
Brecksville, OH 44141-3097
(216) 650-4636

MISTIX Corporation
P.O. Box 85705
San Diego, CA 92138-5705
1-800-283-CAMP

Muskingum Watershed Conservancy District
1319 Third Street, N.W.
P.O. Box 349
New Philadelphia, OH 44663-0349
(216) 343-6647

National Park Service
Midwest Region
1709 Jackson Street
Omaha, NE 68102
(402) 221-3481

North Country National Scenic Trail
National Park Service
P.O. Box 5463
Madison, WI 53705-0463

North Country Trail Association
P.O. Box 311
White Cloud, MI 49349
(616) 689-1912

Wayne-Hoosier National Forests
811 Constitution Avenue
Bedford, Indiana 47421
(812) 275-5987

Index